Blindness and Insight

Paul de Man

BLINDNESS

&

INSIGHT ~ *Essays in*

the Rhetoric of Contemporary Criticism

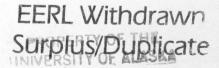

NEW YORK   OXFORD UNIVERSITY PRESS   1971

Cette perpétuelle erreur, qui est
précisément la "vie"...

PROUST

Foreword

The group of essays brought together in this volume claims in no way to be a contribution to the history of criticism or to offer a survey, however sketchy, of the trends that make up present-day literary criticism in Europe. It is concerned with a different problem. Each essay deals with a question of literary understanding but none approaches this question in a systematic way. They were written for specific occasions—conferences, lectures, homages—and reflect interests that are bound to occur to someone whose teaching has been more or less evenly divided between the United States and Europe. The topics were chosen because of a spontaneous, sometimes personal, interest in a particular critic, without trying to present a comprehensive selection. Many essays are by-products of a more extensive study of romantic and post-romantic literature that does not deal with criticism. The recurrent pattern that emerges was established in retrospect and any resemblance to pre-established theories of literary interpretation is entirely coincidental or, in the terminology of the book, blind. I have made no attempt to bring the terminology of the earlier essays up to date and, except for minor changes, have left them as they were originally written.

I stress the somewhat unsystematic aspect of the volume in order to dispel a false impression that could be created by the emphasis on criticism at the expense of general literature. My interest in criticism is subordinate to my interest in primary literary texts. Just as I disclaim any attempt to contribute to a history of modern criticism, I feel equally remote from a science of criticism that would exist as an autonomous discipline. My tentative generalizations are not aimed toward a theory of criticism but toward literary language in general. The usual distinctions between expository writing *on* literature and the "purely" literary language *of* poetry or fiction have been deliberately blurred. The choice of critics who are also novelists or poets, the use of expository critical texts by such poets as Baudelaire or Yeats, the predilection for authors who combine discursive, essayistic writing with the writing of fiction, all tend in this same direction. I am concerned with the distinctive quality that all these modes of writing, as literary texts, have in common and it is toward the preliminary description of this distinctive quality that the essays are oriented.

Why then complicate matters further by choosing to write on critics when one could so easily find less ambivalent examples of literary texts among poets or novelists? The reason is that prior to theorizing about literary language, one has to become aware of the complexities of reading. And since critics are a particularly self-conscious and specialized kind of reader, these complexities are displayed with particular clarity in their work. They do not occur with the same clarity to a spontaneous, non-critical reader who is bound to forget the mediations separating the text from the particular meaning that now captivates his attention. Neither are the complexities of reading easily apparent in a poem or a novel, where they are so deeply embedded in the language that it takes extensive interpretation to bring them to light. Because critics deal more or less openly with the problem of reading, it is a little easier to read a critical text *as text*—i.e. with an awareness of the reading process involved—than to read other literary works in this manner. The study of critical texts, however, can never be an end in itself and has value only as a preliminary to the understanding of literature in general. The problems involved in critical reading reflect the distinctive characteristics of literary language.

The picture of reading that emerges from the examination of a few contemporary critics is not a simple one. In all of them a paradoxical discrepancy appears between the general statements they make about the nature of literature (statements on which they base their critical methods) and the actual results of their interpretations. Their findings about the structure of texts contradict the general conception that they use as their model. Not only do they remain unaware of this discrepancy, but they seem to thrive on it and owe their best insights to the assumptions these insights disprove.

I have tried to document this curious pattern in a number of specific instances. By choosing the critics among writers whose literary perceptiveness lies beyond dispute, I suggest that this pattern of discrepancy, far from being the consequence of individual or collective aberrations, is a constitutive characteristic of literary language in general. A somewhat more systematic formulation of the deluding interplay between text and reader is undertaken in the essay entitled "The Rhetoric of Blindness."

I have not extended the conclusions of the section on criticism to poetry or fiction but I have indicated, in the two concluding essays, how the insight derived from critical practice influences our conception of literary history. If we no longer take for granted that a literary text can be reduced to a finite meaning or set of meanings, but see the act of reading as an endless process in which truth and falsehood are inextricably intertwined, then the prevailing schemes used in literary history (generally derived from genetic models) are no longer applicable. The question of modernity, for example, can no longer be expressed by the usual metaphors of death and rebirth. These metaphors apply to natural objects and to conscious subjects but not to the elusive enigmas that literary texts turn out to be. The two concluding essays make the transition to the exegetic and historical questions raised by our own, post-romantic modernity.

My indebtednesses are too numerous to enumerate. They are particularly conspicuous with regard to the critics I write about, especially when I seem to dispute their assumptions. As a matter of fact, the ungracious relationship between the criticized text and the indebted critic of that text may well be what the book is really about.

P. de M.

Baltimore-Zürich
1970

Acknowledgments

The opening essay was originally delivered as a lecture at the University of Texas and appeared in *Arion* under the title "The Crisis of Contemporary Criticism" (Spring 1967). The essay on the New Criticism was first given as a lecture for the History of Ideas Club at the Johns Hopkins University. "Ludwig Binswanger et le moi poétique" was a contribution to a *Décade* on criticism at Cerisy-la-Salle in Normandy and was printed in the subsequent volume of the proceedings, Ricardou, ed., *Chemins actuels de la critique* (Paris: Plon, 1966). The short piece on Lukács was written for a conference on criticism held at Yale University and later published in *MLN* (December 1966). The study on Blanchot appeared in the special issue of *Critique* on Blanchot ("Circularité de l'interprétation dans la critique de Maurice Blanchot," *Critique*, June 1966). I wrote the next essay for my friend and colleague at the University of Zürich, Georges Poulet; a slightly shortened version appeared in *Critique* (July 1969). The seventh essay, centered on Jacques Derrida's reading of Rousseau, was written for this book. "Literary History and Literary Modernity" was a contribution to a conference on *The Use of Theory in Humanistic Studies* sponsored by *Daedalus* and held at Bellagio in September 1969. "Lyric and Modernity" was delivered at the English Institute during the September 1969 session on the lyric chaired by Professor Reuben A. Brower. Permission to reprint from the various periodicals is gratefully acknowledged.

I have myself translated into English the four essays originally written in French as well as the quotations from various French and German authors.

Contents

Blindness and Insight

I

Criticism and Crisis

When the French poet Stéphane Mallarmé visited Oxford in 1894 to deliver a lecture entitled *La Musique et les lettres* and dealing with the state of French poetry at the time, he exclaimed, with mock sensationalism:

"I am indeed bringing you news. The most surprising news ever. Nothing like it ever happened before. They have tampered with the rules of verse . . . *On a touché au vers*" (Pléiade ed., 643).

In 1970, one might well feel tempted to echo Mallarmé's words, this time with regard not to poetry, but to literary criticism. *On a touché à la critique*. . . . Well-established rules and conventions that governed the discipline of criticism and made it a cornerstone of the intellectual establishment have been so badly tampered with that the entire edifice threatens to collapse. One is tempted to speak of recent developments in Continental criticism in terms of *crisis*. To confine oneself for the moment to purely outward symptoms, the crisis-aspect of the situation is apparent, for instance, in the incredible swiftness with which often conflicting tendencies succeed each other, condemning to immediate obsolescence what

3

might have appeared as the extreme point of avant-gardisme briefly before. Rarely has the dangerous word "new" been used so freely; a few years ago, for very different reasons, there used to be in Paris a *Nouvelle Nouvelle Revue Française*, but today almost every new book that appears inaugurates a new kind of nouvelle nouvelle critique. It is hard to keep up with the names and the trends that succeed each other with bewildering rapidity. Not much more than ten years ago, names such as those of Bachelard, Sartre, Blanchot, or Poulet seemed to be those of daring pioneers, and younger men such as Jean-Pierre Richard or Jean Starobinski proudly considered themselves as continuators of the novel approaches that originated with their immediate predecessors. At that time, the main auxiliary discipline for literary criticism was undoubtedly philosophy. At the Sorbonne, which then as now saw its role primarily as one of conservation and even reaction, the theses considered too bold and experimental to be handled by the chairs of literature would quite naturally find their home among the philosophers. These philosophers were themselves engaged in working out a difficult synthesis between the vitalism of Bergson and the phenomenological method of Husserl; this tendency proved quite congenial to the combined use of the categories of sensation, consciousness and temporality that is prevalent among the literary critics of this group. Today, very little remains, at least on the surface, of this cooperation between phenomenology and literary criticism. Philosophy, in the classical form of which phenomenology was, in France, the most recent manifestation, is out of fashion and has been replaced by the social sciences.

But it is by no means clear which one of the social sciences has taken its place, and the hapless and impatient new new critic is hard put deciding in which discipline he should invest his reading time. For a while, after Lucien Goldman's theses on the sociology of Jansenism in the seventeenth century, it seemed as if sociology was in the lead, and the name of Lukács was being mentioned in Parisian intellectual circles with the same awe that used to surround the figures of Kierkegaard and Hegel a few years earlier. But then Lévi-Strauss' *Tristes tropiques* appeared, and anthropology definitely edged out sociology as the main concern of the literary critic. Hardly had he mastered the difficult terminology of tribal intersubjectivity when linguistics appeared over the horizon with an even more formidable technical jargon. And with the somewhat subterranean influence of Jacques Lacan, psychoanalysis has made a comeback, giving rise to a neo-Freudian rebirth that seems to be quite germane to the concerns of several critics.

This sudden expansion of literary studies outside their own province and into the realm of the social sciences was perhaps long overdue. What is nowadays labeled "structuralism" in France is, on a superficial level, nothing but an attempt to formulate a general methodology of the sciences of man. Literary studies and literary criticism naturally play a certain part in this inquiry. There is nothing particularly new or crisis-like about this. Such attempts to situate literary studies in relation to the social sciences are a commonplace of nineteenth-century thought, from Hegel to Taine and Dilthey. What seems crisis-like is, among outer signs, the sense of urgency, the impatient competitiveness with which the various disciplines vie for leadership.

What interest can this Gallic turbulence have for literary studies in America? The irony of Mallarmé's situation at his Oxford lecture was that his English listeners had little awareness of the emergency by which he claimed to be so disturbed. English prosody had not waited for some rather disreputable foreigners to start tampering with verse; free and blank verse were nothing very new in the country of Shakespeare and Milton, and English literary people thought of the alexandrine as the base supporting the column of the Spenserian stanza rather than as a way of life. They probably had difficulty understanding the rhetoric of crisis that Mallarmé was using, with an ironic slant that would not have been lost in Paris, but that certainly baffled his foreign audience. Similarly, speaking of a crisis in criticism in the United States today, one is likely to appear equally out of tone. Because American criticism is more eclectic, less plagued than its European counterpart by ideology, it is very open to impulses from abroad but less likely to experience them with the same crisis-like intensity. We have some difficulty taking seriously the polemical violence with which methodological issues are being debated in Paris. We can invoke the authority of the best historians to point out that what was considered a crisis in the past often turns out to be a mere ripple, that changes first experienced as upheavals tend to become absorbed in the continuity of much slower movements as soon as the temporal perspective broadens.

This kind of pragmatic common sense is admirable, up to the point where it lures the mind into self-satisfied complacency and puts it irrevocably to sleep. It can always be shown, on all levels of experience, that what other people experience as a crisis is perhaps not even a change; such observations depend to a very large extent on the standpoint of the observer. Historical "changes" are not like changes in nature, and the vocabulary of change and movement as it applies to historical process is a mere metaphor, not devoid of meaning, but without an objective correlative that can unambiguously be pointed to in empirical reality, as when we speak of a change in the weather or a change in a biological organism. No set of arguments, no enumeration of symptoms will ever prove that the present effervescence surrounding literary criticism is in fact a crisis that, for better or worse, is reshaping the critical consciousness of a generation. It remains relevant, however, that these people are experiencing it as a crisis and that they are constantly using the language of crisis in referring to what is taking place. We must take this into account when reflecting on the predicament of others as a preliminary before returning to ourselves.

Again, Mallarmé's text of his Oxford lecture, very closely linked to another prose text of his that was written a little later on the same subject and is entitled *Crise de vers,* can give us a useful hint. Apparently, in these texts, Mallarmé is speaking about the experiments in prosody undertaken by a group of younger poets who call themselves (often without his direct encouragement) his disciples, and whom he designates by name: Henri de Régnier, Moréas, Vielé-Griffin, Gustave Kahn, Charles Morice, Émile Verhaeren, Dujardin, Albert Mockel, and so on. And he pretends to believe that their partial rejection of traditional verse, in favor of free verse forms that he calls "polymorphic," represents a major crisis, the kind of apocalyptic tempest that often reappears as a central symbol in much of his own later poetry. It is obvious, for any historian of French literature, that Mallarmé exaggerates the importance of what is happening around him, to the point of appearing completely misled, not only in the eyes of his more phlegmatic British audience, but in the eyes of future historians as well. The poets he mentions are hardly remembered today, and certainly not praised for the explosive renovation with which Mallarmé seems to credit them. Moreover, one can rightly point out that Mallarmé not only overstates their importance, but that he seems to be blind to the forces within his own time that were indeed to have a lasting effect: he makes only a passing reference to Laforgue, who is somewhat incongruously linked with Henri de Régnier, but fails to mention Rimbaud. In short, Mallarmé seems to be entirely mystified into over-evaluating his own private circle of friends, and his use of the term "crisis" seems to be inspired by propaganda rather than by insight.

It does not take too attentive a reading of the text, however, to show that Mallarmé is in fact well aware of the relative triviality of what his disciples are taking so seriously. He is using them as a screen, a pretext to talk about something that concerns him much more; namely, his own experiments with poetic language. That is what he is referring to when he describes the contemporary condition of poetry as follows: "Orage, lustral; et dans des bouleversements, tout à l'acquit de la génération, récente, l'acte d'écrire se scruta jusqu'en l'origine. Très avant, au moins, quant au point, je le formule;—à savoir s'il y a lieu d'écrire." Freely translated and considerably flattened by filling in the elliptic syntax this becomes: "A tempest cleared the air: the new generation deserves credit for bringing this about. The act of writing scrutinized itself to the point of reflecting on its own origin, or, at any rate, far enough to reach the point where it could ask whether it is necessary for this act to take place." It matters little whether the "recent" generation to which Mallarmé refers indicates his younger disciples or his own contemporaries such as Verlaine, Villiers or even potentially Rimbaud. We know with certainty that something crisis-like was taking place at that moment, making practices and assumptions problematic that had been taken for granted.

We have, to a large extent, lost interest in the actual event that Mallarmé was describing as a crisis, but we have not at all lost interest in a text that pretends to designate a crisis when it is, in fact, itself the crisis to which it refers. For here, as in all of

Mallarmé's later prose and poetic works, the act of writing reflects indeed upon its own origin and opens up a cycle of questions that none of his real successors have been allowed to forget. We can speak of crisis when a "separation" takes place, by self-reflection, between what, in literature, is in conformity with the original intent and what has irrevocably fallen away from this source. Our question in relation to contemporary criticism then becomes: Is criticism indeed engaged in scrutinizing itself to the point of reflecting on its own origin? Is it asking whether it is necessary for the act of criticism to take place?

The matter is still further complicated by the fact that such scrutiny defines, in effect, the act of criticism itself. Even in its most naïve form, that of evaluation, the critical act is concerned with conformity to origin or specificity: when we say of art that it is good or bad, we are in fact judging a certain degree of conformity to an original intent called artistic. We imply that bad art is barely art at all; good art, on the contrary, comes close to our preconceived and implicit notion of what art ought to be. For that reason, the notion of crisis and that of criticism are very closely linked, so much so that one could state that all true criticism occurs in the mode of crisis. To speak of a crisis of criticism is then, to some degree, redundant. In periods that are not periods of crisis, or in individuals bent on avoiding crisis at all cost, there can be all kinds of approaches to literature: historical, philological, psychological, etc., but there can be no criticism. For such periods or individuals will never put the act of writing into question by relating it to its specific intent. The Continental criticism of today is doing just that, and it therefore deserves to be called genuine literary criticism. It will become clear, I hope, that this is not to be considered as an evaluative but as a purely descriptive statement. Whether authentic criticism is a liability or an asset to literary studies as a whole remains an open question. One thing, however, is certain; namely, that literary studies cannot possibly refuse to take cognizance of its existence. It would be as if historians refused to acknowledge the existence of wars because they threaten to interfere with the serenity that is indispensable to an orderly pursuit of their discipline.

The trend in Continental criticism, whether it derives its lan-

guage from sociology, psychoanalysis, ethnology, linguistics, or
even from certain forms of philosophy, can be quickly summarized: it represents a methodologically motivated attack on the
notion that a literary or poetic consciousness is in any way a
privileged consciousness, whose use of language can pretend to
escape, to some degree, from the duplicity, the confusion, the un-
truth that we take for granted in the everyday use of language. We
know that our entire social language is an intricate system of
rhetorical devices designed to escape from the direct expression
of desires that are, in the fullest sense of the term, unnameable—
not because they are ethically shameful (for this would make the
problem a very simple one), but because unmediated expression
is a philosophical impossibility. And we know that the individual
who chose to ignore this fundamental convention would be slated
either for crucifixion, if he were aware, or, if he were naïve,
destined to the total ridicule accorded such heroes as Candide and
all other fools in fiction or in life. The contemporary contribution
to this age-old problem comes by way of a rephrasing of the problem that develops when a consciousness gets involved in interpreting another consciousness, the basic pattern from which there can
be no escape in the social sciences (if there is to be such a thing).
Lévi-Strauss, for instance, starts out from the need to protect anthropologists engaged in the study of a so-called "primitive" society
from the error made by earlier positivistic anthropologists when
they projected upon this society assumptions that remained non-
consciously determined by the inhibitions and shortcomings of
their own social situation. Prior to making any valid statement
about a distant society, the observing subject must be as clear as
possible about his attitude towards his own. He will soon discover,
however, that the only way in which he can accomplish this self-
demystification is by a (comparative) study of his own social self
as it engages in the observation of others, and by becoming aware
of the pattern of distortions that this situation necessarily implies.
The observation and interpretation of others is always also a means
of leading to the observation of the self; true anthropological
knowledge (in the ethnological as well as in the philosophical,
Kantian sense of the term) can only become worthy of being called
knowledge when this alternating process of mutual interpretation

between the two subjects has run its course. Numerous complications arise, because the observing subject is no more constant than the observed, and each time the observer actually succeeds in interpreting his subject he changes it, and changes it all the more as his interpretation comes closer to the truth. But every change of the observed subject requires a subsequent change in the observer, and the oscillating process seems to be endless. Worse, as the oscillation gains in intensity and in truth, it becomes less and less clear who is in fact doing the observing and who is being observed. Both parties tend to fuse into a single subject as the original distance between them disappears. The gravity of this development will at once be clear if I allow myself to shift, for a brief moment, from the anthropological to the psychoanalytical or political model. In the case of a genuine analysis of the psyche, it means that it would no longer be clear who is analyzing and who is being analyzed; consequently the highly embarrassing question arises, who should be paying whom. And on a political level, the equally distressing question as to who should be exploiting whom, is bound to arise.

The need to safeguard reason from what might become a dangerous *vertige,* a dizziness of the mind caught in an infinite regression, prompts a return to a more rational methodology. The fallacy of a finite and single interpretation derives from the postulate of a privileged observer; this leads, in turn, to the endless oscillation of an intersubjective demystification. As an escape from this predicament, one can propose a radical relativism that operates from the most empirically specific to the most loftily general level of human behavior. There are no longer any standpoints that can a priori be considered privileged, no structure that functions validly as a model for other structures, no postulate of ontological hierarchy that can serve as an organizing principle from which particular structures derive in the manner in which a deity can be said to engender man and the world. All structures are, in a sense, equally fallacious and are therefore called myths. But no myth ever has sufficient coherence not to flow back into neighboring myths or even has an identity strong enough to stand out by itself without an arbitrary act of interpretation that defines it. The relative unity of traditional myths always depends on the existence of a privileged point of view to which the method itself denies any status of authenticity. "Contrary to philosophical reflection, which claims to return to the source," writes Claude Lévi-Strauss in *Le Cru et le cuit*, "the reflective activities involved in the structural study of myths deal with light rays that issue from a virtual focal point. . . ." The method aims at preventing this virtual focus from being made into a *real* source of light. The analogy with optics is perhaps misleading, for in literature everything hinges on the existential status of the focal point; and the problem is more complex when it involves the disappearance of the self as a constitutive subject.

These remarks have made the transition from anthropology to the field of language and, finally, of literature. In the act of anthropological intersubjective interpretation, a fundamental discrepancy always prevents the observer from coinciding fully with the consciousness he is observing. The same discrepancy exists in everyday language, in the impossibility of making the actual expression coincide with what has to be expressed, of making the actual sign coincide with what it signifies. It is the distinctive privilege of language to be able to hide meaning behind a misleading sign, as when we hide rage or hatred behind a smile. But it is the distinctive curse of all language, as soon as any kind of interpersonal relation is involved, that it is forced to act this way. The simplest of wishes cannot express itself without hiding behind a screen of language that constitutes a world of intricate intersubjective relationships, all of them potentially inauthentic. In the everyday language of communication, there is no a priori privileged position of sign over meaning or of meaning over sign; the act of interpretation will always again have to establish this relation for the particular case at hand. The interpretation of everyday language is a Sisyphean task, a task without end and without progress, for the other is always free to make what he wants differ from what he says he wants. The methodology of structural anthropology and that of post-Saussurian linguistics thus share the common problem of a built-in discrepancy within the intersubjective relationship. As Lévi-Strauss, in order to protect the rationality of his science, had to come to the conclusion of a myth without an author, so the linguists have to conceive of a meta-language without speaker in order to remain rational.

Literature, presumably, is a form of language, and one can argue that all other art forms, including music, are in fact proto-literary languages. This, indeed, was Mallarmé's thesis in his Oxford lecture, as it is Lévi-Strauss' when he states that the language of music, as a language without speaker, comes closest to being the kind of meta-language of which the linguists are dreaming. If the radical position suggested by Lévi-Strauss is to stand, if the question of structure can only be asked from a point of view that is not that of a privileged subject, then it becomes imperative to show that literature constitutes no exception, that its language is in no sense privileged in terms of unity and truth over everyday forms of language. The task of structuralist literary critics then becomes quite clear: in order to eliminate the constitutive subject, they have to show that the discrepancy between sign and meaning (*signifiant* and *signifié*) prevails in literature in the same manner as in everyday language.

Some contemporary critics have more or less consciously been doing this. Practical criticism, in France and in the United States, functions more and more as a demystification of the belief that literature is a privileged language. The dominant strategy consists of showing that certain claims to authenticity attributed to literature are in fact expressions of a desire that, like all desires, falls prey to the duplicities of expression. The so-called "idealism" of literature is then shown to be an idolatry, a fascination with a false image that mimics the presumed attributes of authenticity when it is in fact just the hollow mask with which a frustrated, defeated consciousness tries to cover up its own negativity.

Perhaps the most specific example of this strategy is the use made by structuralist critics of the historical term "romantic"; the example also has the virtue of revealing the historical scheme within which they are operating, and which is not always openly stated. The fallacy of the belief that, in the language of poetry, sign and meaning can coincide, or at least be related to each other in the free and harmonious balance that we call beauty, is said to be a specifically romantic delusion. The unity of appearance (sign) and idea (meaning)—to use the terminology that one finds indeed among the theoreticians of romanticism when they speak of *Schein* and *Idee*—is said to be a romantic myth embodied in the recurrent topos of the "Beautiful Soul." The *schöne Seele,* a predominant theme of pietistic origin in eighteenth- and nineteenth-century literature, functions indeed as the *figura* of a privileged kind of language. Its outward apparance receives its beauty from an inner glow (or *feu sacré*) to which it is so finely attuned that, far from hiding it from sight, it gives it just the right balance of opacity and transparency, thus allowing the holy fire to shine without burning. The romantic imagination embodies this figure at times in the shape of a person, feminine, masculine or hermaphrodite, and seems to suggest that it exists as an actual, empirical subject: one thinks, for instance, of Rousseau's Julie, of Hölderlin's Diotima, or of the beautiful soul that appears in Hegel's *Phenomenology of the Spirit* and in Goethe's *Wilhelm Meister.*

At this point, it is an irresistible temptation for the demystifying critic, from Voltaire down to the present, to demonstrate that this person, this actual subject, becomes ludicrous when it is transplanted in the fallen world of our facticity. The beautiful soul can be shown to spring from fantasies by means of which the writer sublimates his own shortcomings; it suffices to remove the entity for a moment from the fictional world in which it exists to make it appear even more ridiculous than Candide. Some authors, writing in the wake of the romantic myth, have been well aware of this. One can see how certain developments in nineteenth-century realism, the ironic treatment of the Rousseauistic figure by Stendhal, of the quixotic figure by Flaubert, or of the "poetic" figure by Proust, can be interpreted as a gradual demystification of romantic idealism. This leads to a historical scheme in which romanticism represents, so to speak, the point of maximum delusion in our recent past, whereas the nineteenth and twentieth centuries represent a gradual emerging from this aberration, culminating in the breakthrough of the last decades that inaugurates a new form of insight and lucidity, a cure from the agony of the romantic disease. Refining on what may appear too crude in such a historical scheme, some modern critics transpose this movement within the consciousness of a single writer and show how the development of a novelist can best be understood as a successive process of mystifications and partial demystifications. The process does not necessarily move in one single direction, from delusion to insight; there can be an intricate play of relapses and momentary recoveries. All the same, the fundamental movement of the literary mind espouses the pattern of a demystifying consciousness; literature finally comes into its own, and becomes authentic, when it discovers that the exalted status it claimed for its language was a myth. The function of the critic then naturally becomes coextensive with the intent at demystification that is more or less consciously present in the mind of the author.

This scheme is powerful and cogent, powerful enough, in fact, to go to the root of the matter and consequently to cause a crisis. To reject it convincingly would require elaborate argument. My remarks are meant to indicate some reasons, however, for considering the conception of literature (or literary criticism) as demystification the most dangerous myth of all, while granting that it forces us, in Mallarmé's terms, to scrutinize the act of writing "jusqu'en l'origine."

For reasons of economy, my starting point will have to be oblique, for in the language of polemics the crooked path often travels faster than the straight one. We must ask ourselves if there is not a recurrent epistemological structure that characterizes all statements made in the mood and the rhetoric of crisis. Let me take an example from philosophy. On May 7 and May 10 of 1935, Edmund Husserl, the founder of phenomenology, delivered in Vienna two lectures entitled "Philosophy and the Crisis of European Humanity"; the title was later changed to "The Crisis of European Humanity and Philosophy," to stress the priority of the concept of crisis as Husserl's main concern. The lectures are the first version of what was to become Husserl's most important later work, the treatise entitled *The Crisis of the European Sciences and Transcendental Phenomenology,* now the sixth volume of the complete works edited by Walter Biemel. In these various titles, two words remain constant: the word "crisis" and the word "European"; it is in the interaction of these two concepts that the epistemological structure of the crisis-statement is fully revealed.

Reading this text with the hindsight that stems from more than thirty years of turbulent history, it strikes one as both prophetic and tragic. Much of what is being stated seems relevant today. It is not by a mere freak of language that the key word "demythification" (*Entmythisierung*), that was destined to have such an important career, appears in the text (VI.340.4), although the context in which the term is used, designating what takes place when the superior theoretical man observes the inferior natural man, is highly revealing. There is a very modern note in Husserl's description of philosophy as a process by means of which naïve assumptions are made accessible to consciousness by an act of critical self-understanding. Husserl conceived of philosophy primarily as a self-interpretation by means of which we eliminate what he calls *Selbstverhülltheit,* the tendency of the self to hide from the light it can cast on itself. The universality of philosophical knowledge stems from a persistently reflective attitude that can take philosophy itself for its theme. He describes philosophy as a prolegomenon to a new kind of praxis, a "universal critique of all life and all the goals of life, of all the man-created cultural systems and achievements" and, consequently, "a criticism of man himself (*Kritik der Menschheit selbst*) and of the values by which he is consciously or pre-consciously being governed."

Alerted by this convincing appeal to self-critical vigilance, Husserl's listeners and his present-day readers may well be tempted to turn this philosophical criticism on Husserl's own text, especially on the numerous sections in which philosophy is said to be the historical privilege of European man. Husserl speaks repeatedly of non-European cultures as primitive, prescientific and pre-philosophical, myth-dominated and congenitally incapable of the disinterested distance without which there can be no philosophical meditation. This, although by his own definition philosophy, as unrestricted reflection upon the self, necessarily tends toward a universality that finds its concrete, geographical correlative in the formation of supratribal, supernational communities such as, for instance, Europe. Why this geographical expansion should have chosen to stop, once and forever, at the Atlantic Ocean and at the Caucasus, Husserl does not say. No one could be more open to Lévi-Strauss' criticism of the mystified anthropologist than Husserl when he warns us, with the noblest of intentions, that we should not assume a potential for philosophical attitudes in non-

European cultures. The privileged viewpoint of the post-Hellenic, European consciousness is never for a moment put into question; the crucial, determining examination on which depends Husserl's right to call himself, by his own terms, a philosopher, is in fact never undertaken. As a European, it seems that Husserl escapes from the necessary self-criticism that is prior to all philosophical truth about the self. He is committing precisely the mistake that Rousseau did not commit when he carefully avoided giving his concept of natural man, the basis of his anthropology, any empirical status whatever. Husserl's claim to European supremacy hardly stands in need of criticism today. Since we are speaking of a man of superior good will, it suffices to point to the pathos of such a claim at a moment when Europe was about to destroy itself as center in the name of its unwarranted claim to be the center.

The point, however, transcends the personal situation. Speaking in what was in fact a state of urgent personal and political crisis about a more general form of crisis, Husserl's text reveals with striking clarity the structure of all crisis-determined statements. It establishes an important truth: the fact that philosophical knowledge can only come into being when it is turned back upon itself. But it immediately proceeds, in the very same text, to do the opposite. The rhetoric of crisis states its own truth in the mode of error. It is itself radically blind to the light it emits. It could be shown that the same is true of Mallarmé's *Crise de vers*, which served as our original starting point—although it would be a great deal more complex to demonstrate the self-mystification of as ironical a man as Mallarmé than of as admirably honest a man as Husserl.

Our question, rather, is the following: How does this pattern of self-mystification that accompanies the experience of crisis apply to literary criticism? Husserl was demonstrating the urgent philosophical necessity of putting the privileged European standpoint into question, but remained himself entirely blind to this necessity, behaving in the most unphilosophical way possible at the very moment when he rightly understood the primacy of philosophical over empirical knowledge. He was, in fact, stating the privileged status of philosophy as an authentic language, but withdrawing at once from the demands of this authenticity as it applied to himself. Similarly, demystifying critics are in fact asserting the privileged status of literature as an authentic language, but withdrawing from the implications by cutting themselves off from the source from which they receive their insight.

For the statement about language, that sign and meaning can never coincide, is what is precisely taken for granted in the kind of language we call literary. Literature, unlike everyday language, begins on the far side of this knowledge; it is the only form of language free from the fallacy of unmediated expression. All of us know this, although we know it in the misleading way of a wishful assertion of the opposite. Yet the truth emerges in the foreknowledge we possess of the true nature of literature when we refer to it as *fiction*. All literatures, including the literature of Greece, have always designated themselves as existing in the mode of fiction; in the *Iliad*, when we first encounter Helen, it is as the emblem of the narrator weaving the actual war into the tapestry of a fictional object. Her beauty prefigures the beauty of all future narratives as entities that point to their own fictional nature. The self-reflecting mirror-effect by means of which a work of fiction asserts, by its very existence, its separation from empirical reality, its divergence, as a sign, from a meaning that depends for its existence on the constitutive activity of this sign, characterizes the work of literature in its essence. It is always against the explicit assertion of the writer that readers degrade the fiction by confusing it with a reality from which it has forever taken leave. "Le pays des chimères est en ce monde le seul digne d'être habité," Rousseau has Julie write, "et tel est le néant des choses humaines qu'hors l'Être existant par lui-même, il n'y a rien de beau que ce qui n'est pas" (*La Nouvelle Heloïse*, Pléiade ed. II, 693). One entirely misunderstands this assertion of the priority of fiction over reality, of imagination over perception, if one considers it as the compensatory expression of a shortcoming, of a deficient sense of reality. It is attributed to a fictional character who knows all there is to know of human happiness and who is about to face death with Socratic equanimity. It transcends the notion of a nostalgia or a desire, since it discovers desire as a fundamental pattern of being that discards any possibility of satisfaction. Elsewhere, Rousseau speaks in similar terms of the nothingness of fiction (*le néant de mes chimères*): "If all my dreams had turned into reality, I would still remain unsatisfied: I would have kept on dreaming, imagining, desiring. In myself, I found an unexplainable void that nothing could have filled; a longing of the heart towards another kind of fulfillment of which I could not conceive but of which I nevertheless felt the attraction" (Letter to Malesherbes, Pléiade ed. I, 1140).

These texts can be called romantic, and I have purposely chosen them within the period and the author that many consider the most deluded of all. But one hesitates to use terms such as nostalgia or desire to designate this kind of consciousness, for all nostalgia or desire is desire of something or for someone; here, the consciousness does not result from the absence of something, but consists of the presence of a nothingness. Poetic language names this void with ever-renewed understanding and, like Rousseau's longing, it never tires of naming it again. This persistent naming is what we call literature. In the same manner that the poetic lyric originates in moments of tranquility, in the absence of actual emotions, and then proceeds to invent fictional emotions to create the illusion of recollection, the work of fiction invents fictional subjects to create the illusion of the reality of others. But the fiction is not myth, for it knows and names itself as fiction. It is not a demystification, it is demystified from the start. When modern critics think they are demystifying literature, they are in fact being demystified by it; but since this necessarily occurs in the form of a crisis, they are blind to what takes place within themselves. At the moment that they claim to do away with literature, literature is everywhere; what they call anthropology, linguistics, psychoanalysis is nothing but literature reappearing, like the Hydra's head, in the very spot where it had supposedly been suppressed. The human mind will go through amazing feats of distortion to avoid facing "the nothingness of human matters." In order not to see that the failure lies in the nature of things, one chooses to locate it in the individual, "romantic" subject, and thus retreats behind a historical scheme which, apocalyptic as it may sound, is basically reassuring and bland.

Lévi-Strauss had to give up the notion of subject to safeguard reason. The subject, he said, in fact, is a "foyer virtuel," a mere hypothesis posited by the scientists to give consistency to the behavior of entities. The metaphor in his statement that "the reflective activities [of the structuralists] deal with light that issues from a virtual focal point . . ." stems from the elementary laws of optical refraction. The image is all the more striking since it plays on the confusion between the imaginary loci of the physicist and the *fictional* entities that occur in literary language. The virtual focus is a quasi-objective structure posited to give rational integrity to a process that exists independently of the self. The subject merely fills in, with the dotted line of geometrical construction, what natural reason had not bothered to make explicit; it has a passive and unproblematic role. The "virtual focus" is, strictly speaking, a nothing, but its nothingness concerns us very little, since a mere act of reason suffices to give it a mode of being that leaves the rational order unchallenged. The same is not true of the imaginary source of fiction. Here the human self has experienced the void within itself and the invented fiction, far from filling the void, asserts itself as pure nothingness, *our* nothingness stated and restated by a subject that is the agent of its own instability. Lévi-Strauss' suppression of the subject is perfectly legitimate as an attempt to protect the scientific status of ethnology; by the same token, however, it leads directly into the larger question of the ontological status of the self. From this point on, a philosophical anthropology would be inconceivable without the consideration of literature as a primary source of knowledge.

II

Form and Intent in the
American New Criticism

Not longer than ten years ago, a comparison of American and European criticism would in all likelihood have had to focus on the differences between a stylistic and a historical approach to literature. In evaluating what American criticism stood to gain from a closer contact with Europe, one would have stressed the balance achieved in some of the best European works between historical knowledge and a genuine feeling for literary form. For reasons that are themselves part of history, the same synthesis was rarely achieved in America; the intellectual history that originated with Lovejoy and that could have combined a European sense of history with an American sense of form was the exception rather than the norm. The predominant influence, that of the New Criticism, was never able to overcome the anti-historical bias that presided over its beginnings. This inability certainly was one of the reasons that prevented it from making major contributions, in spite of considerable methodological originality and refinement.

One can think of several ways in which a closer contact with European methods could have contributed to a broadening of the New Critical approach. Opportunities for such contacts were never lacking. After all, some of the most representative European historians, as well as some of the best practitioners of contemporary stylistics, spent much time in America: one thinks of Erich Auerbach, Leo Spitzer, Georges Poulet, Damaso Alonso, Roman Jakobson, and several others. That their influence remained by and large confined to their national field of specialization indicates how difficult it is to break down the barriers that, in our universities, keep the various departments separated from each other. Perhaps American formalism needed this isolation to come fully into its own. Whatever the case may be, even when the influence of the New Criticism reached its height, it remained confined within its original boundaries and was allowed to do so without being seriously challenged.

Such a challenge could have come from various sources, without really having to upset the traditional patterns of literary studies. But today, it is too late to bring about this kind of encounter. One can regret this, yet an analysis of the causes that prevented the confrontation is purely academic. Over the last five years, a far-reaching change has taken place here and abroad, putting the entire question of literary studies in a different perspective. Whether American or European, whether oriented toward form or toward history, the main critical approaches of the last decades were all founded on the implicit assumption that literature is an autonomous activity of the mind, a distinctive way of being in the world to be understood in terms of its own purposes and intentions. This autonomy is now again being successfully challenged. Contemporary French structuralism applies methodological patterns derived from the social sciences (especially anthropology and linguistics) to the study of literature; similar tendencies can be observed in the renewed interest of American critics in sociological, political, and psychological considerations that had never ceased to be present, but had been kept in the background. Ironically enough, the long-awaited unification of European and American criticism seems to be coming about, albeit in the form of a radical questioning of the autonomy of literature as an aesthetic activity.

The trend can be welcomed, though not uncritically. It forces a long overdue re-examination of the assumptions on which the position of autonomy was founded, for it is not at all certain that this position had been well understood by the American formalists; their conviction may very well have been founded on preconceptions that were themselves derived from non-literary models. The kind of autonomy to be found in literary works is certainly far from self-evident; it has to be redefined before we can ask whether it is being challenged in the name of regressive trends, methods that apply to less rigorous modes of consciousness than those at work in literary language. As one of the questions that can give insight into this matter, the nature of the relationship between form and intent provides a possible way of approach.

We can take as a point of departure a remark of the English semanticist Stephen Ullmann in a work on the stylistics of French fiction. Ullmann is led to a discussion of the method of Leo Spitzer and speaks of the rebuke that is frequently addressed to Spitzer; namely, that his apparently objective philological analyses are, in fact, *a posteriori* rationalizations of emotional convictions that he held long beforehand. Ullmann writes:

> Professor Spitzer has strongly repudiated this allegation; but even if it is true, it does not really affect the value of the method. As long as the demonstration is conclusive, it surely does not matter in what order the various steps were taken; the main point is that a link has been established between a stylistic peculiarity, its root in the author's psyche, and other manifestations of the same mental factor. The great merit of Spitzer's procedure is indeed that it has lifted stylistic facts out of their isolation and has related them to other aspects of the writer's experience and activity.[1]

Interpreted in a certain way—which is not necessarily how Mr. Ullmann intends it—this affirmation postulates a continuity between the initial subjective experience of the writer and characteristics that belong to the surface dimensions of language—such as properties of sound, of meter, or even of imagery, all of which belong to the domain of sensory experience. This continuity im-

1. Stephen Ullmann, *Style in the French Novel* (Cambridge, Eng., 1957), pp. 28–29.

plies a debatable presupposition about the nature of literary language. The formula is tempting for it seems to dispense with adventurous inquiries that reach into the darker areas of human subjectivity and to leave us instead in a clear and precise zone in which properties can be observed and even measured. But can we take this continuity between depth and surface, between style and theme, for granted? Is it not rather the most problematic issue with which the theory of poetry will have to deal?

In another work—historical and thematic in scope rather than purely stylistic—Erich Auerbach's *Mimesis*, the author, in speaking of the tension that exists in Western literature between the Biblical and the Hellenic traditions, characterizes Western literature as a "struggle between sensory appearance and meaning (Kampf zwischen sinnlicher Erscheinung und Bedeutung) which pervades the Christian sense of reality from the beginning and, in truth, in its totality." [2] And, as is clear from the context, the "meaning" to which Auerbach alludes here is not just the immediate semantic *donnée* of a text but the deeper inward experience that determines the choice and articulation of the themes. However, if this is indeed the case, the study of the "sensory appearances" that is the field of stylistics can never lead to the real meaning of the themes since both, at least in Western literature, are separated by a radical discontinuity that no dialectic is able to bridge. It would be of the utmost importance, in that case, to know whether Leo Spitzer has taken a subjective or a sensory element for his point of departure since we would end up, in each case, in the opposite camp.

It is easy to see to what species of entities Ullmann's description does apply. Certain entities exist the full meaning of which can be said to be equal to the totality of their sensory appearances. For an ideal perception, entirely devoid of complications resulting from the interference of the imagination, the "meaning" of "stone" could only refer to a totality of sensory appearances. The same applies to all natural objects. But even the most purely intuitive consciousness could never conceive of the significance of an object such as, for instance, a chair, without including in the description

2. Erich Auerbach, *Mimesis* (Bern, 1946), Chapter II, p. 55.

an allusion to the *use* to which it is put; the most rigorous description of the perceptions of the object "chair" would remain meaningless if one does not organize them in function of the potential act that defines the object; namely, that it is destined to be sat on. The potential act of sitting down is a constitutive part of the object. If it were absent, the object could not be conceived in its totality. The difference between the stone and the chair distinguishes a natural object from an intentional object. The intentional object requires a reference to a specific act as constitutive of its mode of being. By asserting *a priori,* as in Ullmann's text, that, in literary language, the meaning is equal to the totality of the sensory appearances, one postulates in fact that the language of literature is of the same order, ontologically speaking, as a natural object. The intentional factor has been bypassed.

A clarification of the notion of "intent" is of great importance for an evaluation of American criticism, for at the rare moments when the New Critics consented to express themselves theoretically, the notion of intent always played a prominent part, although it was mostly a negative one. Wimsatt and Beardsley coined the expression "intentional fallacy" as far back as 1942 and this formula, better than any other, delimits the horizon within which this criticism has operated. The expression was developed later on by Wimsatt in his book *The Verbal Icon*, where it is used to assert the autonomy and the unity of the poetic consciousness. Wimsatt wants to defend the province of poetry against the intrusion of crude deterministic systems, historical or psychological, that oversimplify the complex relationship between theme and style. And he focuses on the concept of intention as the breach through which these foreign bodies reach into the poetic domain. But, in so doing, he allows us to observe the very moment at which his concern with autonomy, most legitimate in itself, leads him into contradictory assumptions about the ontological status of the work of literature. Too sensitive an aesthetician to distort things altogether, Wimsatt writes at first: "the poem conceived as a thing in between the poet and the audience is, of course, an abstraction. The poem is an act"—a statement to which an intentional theory of poetry would gladly subscribe. Then Wimsatt continues: "But if we are to lay hold of the poetic act to comprehend and evaluate it, and if it has to pass current as critical object, it must be hypostatized." [3]

If such a hypostasis, which changes the literary act into a literary object by the suppression of its intentional character, is not only possible but necessary in order to allow for a critical description, then we have not left the world in which the status of literary language is similar to that of a natural object. This assumption rests on a misunderstanding of the nature of intentionality. "Intent" is seen, by analogy with a physical model, as a transfer of a psychic or mental content that exists in the mind of the poet to the mind of a reader, somewhat as one would pour wine from a jar into a glass. A certain content has to be transferred elsewhere, and the energy necessary to effect the transfer has to come from an outside source called intention. This is to ignore that the concept of intentionality is neither physcial nor psychological in its nature, but structural, involving the activity of a subject regardless of its empirical concerns, except as far as they relate to the intentionality of the structure. The structural intentionality determines the relationship between the components of the resulting object in all its parts, but the relationship of the particular state of mind of the person engaged in the act of structurization to the structured object is altogether contingent. The structure of the chair is determined in all its components by the fact that it is destined to be sat on, but this structure in no way depends on the state of mind of the carpenter who is in the process of assembling its parts. The case of the work of literature is of course more complex, yet here also, the intentionality of the act, far from threatening the unity of the poetic entity, more definitely establishes this unity.

The rejection of intentionality, by which Wimsatt formulated theoretically what other New Critics were practicing, has proven to be remarkably tenacious. In *The Anatomy of Criticism,* Northrop Frye still refers to the "intentional fallacy" as one of the methodological cornerstones of his system of archetypal rhetorical categories. His formulation seems to be closer to Wimsatt's "act" than to his hypostatized "thing." Frye sees the structure of an inten-

3. William Wimsatt, *The Verbal Icon* (Lexington, Ky., 1954), Chapter I, p. xvii.

tional act as analogous to that of taking aim, as when an object is taken for a target by a weapon directed toward it.[4] He concludes that this type of structure belongs to discursive language which "aims" for the exact relationship and not to poetic language which does not "aim" at anything, being tautologically itself; that is to say, entirely autonomous and without exterior referent. This part of Frye's theory—which hardly detracts from the suggestive value of his further classifications—is founded on a misunderstanding of intentional language and, be it said in passing, of discursive language as well. Up to a point, the act of taking aim provides a correct model for an intentional act, provided an important distinction is made. When a hunter takes aim at a rabbit, we may presume his intention is to eat or to sell the rabbit and, in that case the act of taking aim is subordinated to another intention that exists beyond the act itself. But when he takes aim at an artificial target, his act has no other intention than aim-taking for its own sake and constitutes a perfectly closed and autonomous structure. The act reflects back upon itself and remains circumscribed within the range of its own intent. This is indeed a proper way of distinguishing between different intentional objects such as the tool (the gun that takes aim at the rabbit) and the toy (the gun that takes aim at a clay pipe). The aesthetic entity definitely belongs to the same class as the toy, as Kant and Schiller knew well before Huizinga. In failing to make this distinction, Northrop Frye falls into exactly the same error as Wimsatt and reifies the literary entity into a natural object: with the added danger, moreover, that put in less ironic hands than his own, his theory could cause much more extensive damage. A formalist such as Wimsatt hypostatizes only the particular text on which he is working, but a literal minded disciple of a mythologist like Frye could go a lot further. He is given license to order and classify the whole of literature into one single thing which, even though circular, would nevertheless be a gigantic cadaver. Frye's formula defining all literary creation as "an activity whose intention it is to abolish intention"[5] is only sound if it is allowed to remain forever suspended as an eternal intent.

A truly systematic study of the main formalist critics in the

4. Northrop Frye, *The Anatomy of Criticism* (Princeton, 1957), p. 86.
5. *Ibid.* p. 89.

English language during the last thirty years would always reveal the more or less deliberate rejection of the principle of intentionality. The result would be a hardening of the text into a sheer surface that prevents the stylistic analysis from penetrating beyond the sensory appearances to perceive this "struggle with meaning" of which all criticism, including the criticism of forms, should give an account. For surfaces also remain concealed when they are being artificially separated from the depth that supports them. The partial failure of American formalism, which has not produced works of major magnitude, is due to its lack of awareness of the intentional structure of literary form.

Yet this criticism has merits that prevail despite the weakness of its theoretical foundations. The French critic, Jean-Pierre Richard, alludes to these merits when he writes defensively in the introduction to his study of Mallarmé that "the reproach [of destroying the formal structure of the work] will especially be made by English and American critics for whom, as is well known, the objective and architectural reality of particular works is of the utmost importance." [6] It is true that American textual interpretation and "close reading" have perfected techniques that allow for considerable refinement in catching the details and nuances of literary expression. They study texts as "forms," as groupings from which the constitutive parts cannot be isolated or separated. This gives a sense of context that is often lacking in French or in German interpretations.

But are we not confronted here with a flagrant contradiction? On the one hand, we blame American criticism for considering literary texts as if they were natural objects but, on the other hand, we praise it for possessing a sense of formal unity that belongs precisely to a living and natural organism. Is not this sense of the unity of forms being supported by the large metaphor of the analogy between language and a living organism, a metaphor that shapes a great deal of nineteenth-century poetry and thought? One could even find historical confirmation of this filiation in the line that links, especially by way of I. A. Richards and Whitehead, the structural formalism of the New Critics to the "organic" im-

6. Jean-Pierre Richard, *L'Univers imaginaire de Mallarmé* (Paris, 1961), p. 31.

agination so dear to Coleridge. The introduction of the principle
of intentionality would imperil the organic analogy and lead to a
loss of the sense of form; hence the understandable need of the
New Critics to protect their greatest source of strength.

It should be remembered that, going back to Coleridge himself,
what he called the "esemplastic" power of the imagination was
not unambiguously founded on a participation of consciousness
in the natural energy of the cosmos. M. H. Abrams, in *The Mirror
and the Lamp,* rightly insists on the importance of free will in
Coleridge. "Coleridge," he writes, "though admitting an unconscious component in invention, was determined to demonstrate
that a poet like Shakespeare 'never wrote anything without design.'
What the plant is by an act not its own and unconsciously, Coleridge exhorts us 'that must thou *make* thyself to become'" [7] And,
in *La Métamorphose du cercle,* Georges Poulet, speaking of Coleridge's sense of form, insists that it results from "the explicit action
of our will" which "imposes its law and unique form upon the
poetic universe." [8] This is to say that the structural power of the
poetic imagination is not founded on an analogy with nature, but
that it is intentional. Abrams perceives this very well when he
comments that Coleridge's notion of free will "runs counter, it
would appear, to an inherent tendency of his elected analogue." [9]

The ambivalence reappears among modern disciples of Coleridge, in a curious discrepancy between their theoretical assumptions and their practical results. As it refines its interpretations
more and more, American criticism does not discover a single meaning, but a plurality of significations that can be radically opposed
to each other. Instead of revealing a continuity affiliated with the
coherence of the natural world, it takes us into a discontinuous
world of reflective irony and ambiguity. Almost in spite of itself,
it pushes the interpretative process so far that the analogy between
the organic world and the language of poetry finally explodes. This
unitarian criticism finally becomes a criticism of ambiguity, an
ironic reflection on the absence of the unity it had postulated.

But from where then does the contextual unity, which the

7. M. H. Abrams, *The Mirror and the Lamp* (New York, 1953), pp. 173–74.
8. Georges Poulet, *La Métamorphose du cercle* (Paris, 1961), p. 154.
9. Abrams, *op. cit.* p. 174.

study of texts reconfirms over and over again and to which American criticism owes its effectiveness, stem? Is it not rather that this unity—which is in fact a semi-circularity—resides not in the poetic text as such, but in the act of interpreting this text? The circle we find here and which is called "form" does not stem from an analogy between the text and natural things, but constitutes the hermeneutic circle mentioned by Spitzer[10] of which the history has been traced by Gadamer in *Wahrheit und Methode*[11] and whose ontological significance is at the basis of Heidegger's treatise *Sein und Zeit*.

What happened in American criticism could then be explained as follows: because such patient and delicate attention was paid to the reading of forms, the critics pragmatically entered into the hermeneutic circle of interpretation, mistaking it for the organic circularity of natural processes. This happened quite spontaneously, for Spitzer's influence at the time of the New Criticism was confined to a small area, and Heidegger's influence was nonexistent.

Only some aspects of Heidegger's theory of hermeneutic circularity have to be stressed here. It combines in fact two equally important ideas. The first has to do with the epistemological nature of all interpretation. Contrary to what happens in the physical sciences, the interpretation of an intentional act or an intentional object always implies an *understanding* of the intent. Like scientific laws, interpretation is in fact a generalization that expands the range of applicability of a statement to a wider area. But the nature of the generalization is altogether different from what is most frequently encountered in the natural sciences. There we are concerned with the predictability, the measurement, or the mode of determination of a given phenomenon, but we do not claim in any way to understand it. To interpret an intent, however, can only mean to understand it. No new set of relationships is added to an existing reality, but relationships *that were already there* are being disclosed, not only in themselves (like the events of nature) but as they exist *for us*. We can only understand that which is in

10. Leo Spitzer, *A Method of Interpreting Literature* (Northampton, Mass., 1949).
11. Hans Georg Gadamer, *Wahrheit und Methode* (Tübingen, 1960).

a sense already given to us and already known, albeit in a fragmentary, inauthentic way that cannot be called unconscious. Heidegger calls this the *Forhabe*, the forestructure of all understanding.

> This is a fact [he writes], that has always been remarked, even if only in the area of derivative ways of understanding and interpretation, such as philological interpretation. . . .
>
> Scientific knowledge demands the rigors of demonstration for its justification. In a scientific proof, we may not presuppose what it is our task to demonstrate. But if interpretation must in any case operate in the area of what is already understood, and if it must feed on this understanding, how can it achieve any scientific results without moving in a circle? . . . Yet, according to the most elementary rules of logic, this circle is a *circulus vitiosus*. But if we think this to be a vicious circle and try to avoid it, even if we merely suspect it of being an imperfection, then the act of understanding has been entirely misunderstood. . . . If the basic conditions that make interpretation possible are to be fulfilled, we must recognize from the start the circumstances under which it can be performed. What is decisive is not to get out of the circle but to come into it in the right way. The circle of understanding is not an orbit in which any random kind of knowledge is allowed to move; it is the expression of the existential forestructure of *Dasein* itself. . . . In the circle is hidden a positive possibility of the most primordial kind of knowledge.[12]

For the interpreter of a poetic text, this foreknowledge is the text itself. Once he understands the text, the implicit knowledge becomes explicit and discloses what was already there in full light. Far from being something added to the text, the elucidating commentary simply tries to reach the text itself, whose full richness is there at the start. Ultimately, the ideal commentary would indeed become superfluous and merely allow the text to stand fully revealed. But it goes without saying that this ideal commentary can never exist as such. When Heidegger, in his foreword to his commentaries on the poetry of Hölderlin, claims to write from the standpoint of the ideal commentator, his claim is disquieting

12. Martin Heidegger, *Sein und Zeit* (1927), I, Chapter V.

because it goes against the temporal structure of the hermeneutic process. The implicit foreknowledge is always temporally ahead of the explicit interpretative statement that tries to catch up with it.

The notion of the hermeneutic circle is not introduced by Heidegger in connection with poetry or the interpretation of poetry, but applied to language in general. All language is, to some extent, involved in interpretation, though all language certainly does not achieve understanding. Here the second element of the hermeneutic process comes into play: the notion of circularity or totality. Only when understanding has been achieved does the circle seem to close and only then is the foreknowing structure of the act of interpretation fully revealed. True understanding always implies a certain degree of totality; without it, no contact could be established with a foreknowledge that it can never reach, but of which it can be more or less lucidly aware. The fact that poetic language, unlike ordinary language, possesses what we call "form" indicates that it has reached this point. In interpreting poetic language, and especially in revealing its "form," the critic is therefore dealing with a privileged language: a language engaged in its highest intent and tending toward the fullest possible self-understanding. The critical interpretation is oriented toward a consciousness which is itself engaged in an act of total interpretation. The relationship between author and critic does not designate a difference in the type of activity involved, since no fundamental discontinuity exists between two acts that both aim at full understanding; the difference is primarily temporal in kind. Poetry is the foreknowledge of criticism. Far from changing or distorting it, criticism merely discloses poetry for what it is.

Literary "form" is the result of the dialectic interplay between the prefigurative structure of the foreknowledge and the intent at totality of the interpretative process. This dialectic is difficult to grasp. The idea of totality suggests closed forms that strive for ordered and consistent systems and have an almost irresistible tendency to transform themselves into objective structures. Yet, the temporal factor, so persistently forgotten, should remind us that the form is never anything but a process on the way to its completion. The completed form never exists as a concrete aspect of the work that could coincide with a sensorial or semantic dimen-

sion of the language. It is constituted in the mind of the interpreter as the work discloses itself in response to his questioning.
But this dialogue between work and interpreter is endless. The
hermeneutic understanding is always, by its very nature, lagging
behind: to understand something is to realize that one had always
known it, but, at the same time, to face the mystery of this hidden
knowledge. Understanding can be called complete only when it
becomes aware of its own temporal predicament and realizes that
the horizon within which the totalization can take place is time
itself. The act of understanding is a temporal act that has its own
history, but this history forever eludes totalization. Whenever the
circle seems to close, one has merely ascended or descended one
more step on Mallarmé's "spirale vertigineuse conséquente."

The lesson to be derived from the evolution of American formalist criticism is twofold. It reaffirms first of all the necessary presence
of a totalizing principle as the guiding impulse of the critical
process. In the New Criticism, this principle consisted of a purely
empirical notion of the integrity of literary form, yet the mere
presence of such a principle could lead to the disclosure of distinctive structures of literary language (such as ambiguity and irony)
although these structures contradict the very premises on which
the New Criticism was founded. Second, the rejection of the
principle of intentionality, dismissed as fallacious, prevented the
integration of these discoveries within a truly coherent theory of
literary form. The ambivalence of American formalism is such
that it was bound to lead to a state of paralysis. The problem remains how to formulate the mode of totalization that applies to
literary language and that allows for a description of its distinctive
aspects.

Some similarities can be pointed out between the successes and
the shortcomings of the American New Criticism and corresponding developments in present-day French criticism. The danger of
a reification of the form also seems to threaten the declared ob-
jectivism of several structuralist interpreters of literature. Yet the
theoretical foundations of the two trends have by now moved in
very different directions. In structuralism the loss of the intentional
factor does not result from a debatable identification of language

with the organic world but is due to the suppression of the constitutive subject. The consequences of this suppression reach much
further than in the relatively harmless case of an organicist formalism. A material analogism, as one finds it in the criticism of
Bachelard or of Jean-Pierre Richard, can leave the play of the
poetic imagination quite free. As long as the theoretical assumptions remain weak and loose, the hermeneutic process can take
place more or less unhampered. But the theoretical assumptions
that underlie the methods of structuralism are a great deal more
powerful and consistent. They cannot be dealt with in the course
of a single brief essay.

The critical examination of the structuralist premises will have
to focus on the same set of problems that appeared in the discussion
of formalism: the existence and the nature of the constitutive subject, the temporal structure of the act of interpretation, the necessity for a distinctively literary mode of totalization. It could be
that, in a legitimate desire to react against reductive ways of
thought, the structuralists have bypassed or oversimplified some of
these questions.[13]

In the first critical reactions to arise in response to the structuralist challenge, it is primarily the question of the subject that has
been stressed. Thus Serge Doubrovsky, in the first volume of a
general study on modern French criticism, re-establishes the link
between literary totality and the intent of the writer or subject.
This intent is conceived in Sartrian terms, with a definite awareness of the temporal complexities involved in the process of interpretation. It is doubtful, however, if Doubrovsky remains faithful
to the demands of literary language when he defines its intentionality as the act of an individual "projecting the original relations
between man and reality, the total sense of the human condition,
on the level of the imagination (le plan de l'imaginaire)."[14]
What is this "plan de l'imaginaire" that seems to exist by itself,
independently of language, and why would we need to "project"
ourselves upon it? Doubrovsky answers these questions by referring
to the theories of perception contained in the work of Merleau-
Ponty. He describes all expression as being at the same time dis-

13. The question is discussed in more detail in Chapter VII of this study.
14. Serge Doubrovsky, *Pourquoi la nouvelle critique?* (Paris, 1966), p. 193.

closure as well as dissimulation; the function of art and of literature would be to reveal the reality that is hidden as well as that which is visible. The world of the imagination then becomes a more complete, more totalized reality than that of everyday experience, a three-dimensional reality that would add a factor of depth to the flat surface with which we are usually confronted. Art would be the expression of a completed reality, a kind of over-perception which, as in the famous Rilke poem on the "Archaic Torso of Apollo" would allow us to see things in their completeness and so "change our lives."

The reference to Merleau-Ponty reveals that Doubrovsky has chosen perception as a model for his description of the literary act. And what characterizes perception for Merleau-Ponty is that the intent and the content of the act can be co-extensive.[15] Not only does Doubrovsky accept this essentially positive concept of perception with much less dialectical anxiety than his master, but he extends it at once to include all facets of our relationships toward the world. From being a model for the act of literary invention, perception is extended to coincide in its structure with the entirety of the existential project. It makes our entire existence benefit from the plenitude of an original act, the cogito "I percieve, therefore, I am" experienced as an unquestionable assertion of being. Consequently, the real and the imaginary, the life and the work, history and transcendence, literature and criticism, are all harmoniously integrated in an infinite extension of the perfect unity that stands at the beginning of things.

In so doing, Doubrovsky pushes Merleau-Ponty's thought far beyond its prudent limits. The author of *The Phenomenology of Perception* had sketched the outline of a theory of plastic form in the late essay, *Eye and Mind,* but he refrained from extending his theory to include literary language. It would have been difficult for him to do so, for literature bears little resemblance to perception, and less still to this over-perception of which Doubrovsky is dreaming. It does not fulfill a plenitude but originates in the void that separates intent from reality. The imagination takes its flight only after the void, the inauthenticity of the existential

15. Maurice Merleau-Ponty, *Phénoménologie de la perception* (Paris, 1952), III, Chapter I, "Le cogito."

project has been revealed; literature begins where the existential demystification ends and the critic has no need to linger over this preliminary stage. Considerations of the actual and historical existence of writers are a waste of time from a critical viewpoint. These regressive stages can only reveal an emptiness of which the writer himself is well aware when he begins to write. Many great writers have described the loss of reality that marks the beginning of poetic states of mind, as when, in a famous poem by Baudelaire,

> . . . palais neufs, échafaudages, blocs,
> Vieux faubourgs, tout pour moi devient allégorie. . . .

This "allegorical" dimension, which appears in the work of all genuine writers and constitutes the real depth of literary insight could never be reached by a method like that of Serge Doubrovsky, for it originates on the far side of the existential project. The critic who has written some of the most perceptive pages on Baudelaire, the German essayist Walter Benjamin, knew this very well when he defined allegory as a void "that signifies precisely the non-being of what it represents." We are far removed from the plenitude of perception that Doubrovsky attributes to Merleau-Ponty. But we are much closer to the process of negative totalization that American criticism discovered when it penetrated more or less unwittingly into the temporal labyrinth of interpretation.

III

Ludwig Binswanger and the
Sublimation of the Self

       The methodological questions that are being debated in some sectors of modern German criticism are often centered on the same problems as in France or in America, although the terminology and the historical background are different enough to make direct contact very difficult. It would be impossible moreover to sketch a clear and concise summary that would do justice to the complexity of the various critical trends that have emerged in the German academic and literary world of the last decades. These trends are less centralized than in France, and their diversity reflects a set of historical and sociological conditions that requires detailed analysis. We prefer to use one specific writer as an example of the problem that concerns us: the relationship, in the critical act, between the consciousness of the author and that of the interpreter. This will also allow us to introduce the name of Ludwig Binswanger—a figure well known in the world of psychiatry and of existential philosophy, but whose contribution to literary theory has received too little attention. The work of this Swiss psychiatrist has several ramifications of interest to contemporary

36

criticism. We are referring in particular to an essay entitled *Hendrik Ibsen und das Problem der Selbstrealisation in der Kunst,* which appeared in 1949 and which we are using, in this essay, as our basic text.

We can take for our point of departure a remark of the French philosopher Michel Foucault in a recent and ambitious book entitled *Les Mots et les choses.* Foucault speaks of the changes that introduce radical discontinuities in the history of consciousness, such as the articulation he sees appear at the end of the eighteenth century when the idea of consciousness as representation begins to be challenged. Reflecting on the nature of the event and on the law that governs such mutations, he writes:

> For a study of the origins and the history of knowledge (une archéologie du savoir) that wants to proceed by rigorous analysis, this deep breach in the existing continuities could not be "explained" or even designated in the vocabulary of a single intellectual discipline. It is a radical event that spreads over the entire visible surface of our knowledge and of which the symptoms, the shocks and the consequences can be traced in great detail. Only thought understanding itself at the root of its own history could safely establish what the singular truth of this event may have been. But an "archaeology" of knowledge must be satisfied with describing the observable manifestations of the event. . . . (L'archéologie doit parcourir l'évènement selon sa disposition manifeste.)[1]

Two possible attitudes are being suggested here in dealing with the problem of the constitutive power of consciousness—for this is indeed what we are dealing with in speaking of consciousness as having a history, as being capable of changing its own mode of action. Advocated by Foucault, the first will describe the outward signs of the transformations when they occur within manifest forms of existence; hence Foucault's orientation toward disciplines such as economics, politics, sociology, or, in general, any structure that operates on the level of the empirical and the concrete. The other attitude would be precisely that of "thought understanding itself at the root of its own history." It seems that, for Foucault

1. Michel Foucault, *Les Mots et les choses* (Paris, 1966), p. 230.

this second road is no longer accessible and that the past can only be studied as a network of surface-structures, without any attempt to understand the movements of consciousness from the inside in an act of self-reflection. What Foucault calls an *archaeology* of ideas (in deliberate contrast to a *history* of ideas) takes for its object the ruins of the edifice erected in the course of the nineteenth century by the humanistic philosophical anthropology on which our historical and interpretative methods are founded.

Certain aspects of contemporary German thought may appear closely related to such an attitude, especially in its attempt to move beyond the classical "science of man" derived from Kant. This certainly was the case with Nietzsche; closer to our own time and to our concern with literary problems, it is also the case with the criticism that Heidegger and others have addressed to the anthropological historicism of Dilthey, whose influence on German literary studies still persists today. But the similarity stops there, for phenomenological and Heideggerian trends, especially in their application to literature, lead into altogether different directions than Foucault's archaeology of intellectual structures. They tend instead toward a deepening investigation of the question of the self which remains the starting-point of the attempt at a philosophical understanding of existence. But this does not mean that these trends persist in taking a preconceived notion of "man" for granted. Heidegger especially, ever since *Sein und Zeit,* has consistently denied that his undertaking leads toward a philosophical anthropology in the Kantian sense of the term. His purpose is directed toward a fundamental ontology, not toward a science of empirical man. The question of the self is not asked in terms of a more or less elaborated conception of consciousness, whether this conception be empirical, psychological, or even, as for Dilthey, historical. It is asked only in terms of its relationship to the constitutive categories of being. This reductive rigor, which wants to see the self only as it stands out against the background of more fundamental categories, requires a difficult and constant effort of interpretative vigilance. We fall prey to an almost irresistible tendency to relapse unwittingly into the concerns of the self as they exist in the empirical world. Binswanger's own work, despite the strong influence of Heidegger, provides a good instance of precisely this kind of relapse. Part of its interest stems from the insight it gives into the very process of falling-back. It is often in connection with literature, where the problem of the self is particularly delicate, that this onto-ontological confusion occurs in the most revealing manner. However, such confusions are in the long run more instructive than the peremptory dismissal of the question of the subject on historical grounds, leading to the *a priori* rejection of all attempts to elaborate a phenomenology of consciousness as a constitutive act.

In the study of literature, the question of the self appears in a bewildering network of often contradictory relationships among a plurality of subjects. It appears first of all, as in the Third Critique of Kant, in the act of judgment that takes place in the mind of the reader; it appears next in the apparently intersubjective relationships that are established between the author and the reader; it governs the intentional relationship that exists, within the work, between the constitutive subject and the constituted language; it can be sought, finally, in the relationship that the subject establishes, through the mediation of the work, with itself. From the start, we have at least four possible and distinct types of self: the self that judges, the self that reads, the self that writes, and the self that reads itself. The question of finding the common level on which all these selves meet and thus of establishing the unity of a literary consciousness stands at the beginning of the main methodological difficulties that plague literary studies.

The title of the essay by Ludwig Binswanger that we have chosen for our text clearly indicates that we are dealing with the fourth type of self, that of the author as he is changed and interpreted by his own work. The essay is entitled, "Hendrik Ibsen and the Problem of the Development of the Self *in art*" (Das Problem der Selbstrealisation *in der Kunst*). The self under development is that of Ibsen as it was shaped by his deliberate choice to carry out the work to its final end. For that purpose, Ibsen had to relinquish the self that he had inherited, so to speak, at birth; he had to leave behind the set of particular circumstances that defined his initial situation in the world: family, place of birth, psychological and sociological conditions, all had to fade before the project of a future literary work. The original Ibsen had to undergo a fundamental change in order to grow and to find his genuine dimension. For Binswanger the literary enterprise can nowhere be distinguished from the project of self-realization. Both are so intimately bound up with each other that the critic can move back and forth between the realm of the self and that of the work without any apparent tension. The expansion of the self seems to occur in and probably by means of the work. The authenticating function of the work that "elevates" the writer above his original identity is so fundamentally implicit in Binswanger's thought that he takes it entirely for granted, without feeling called upon to state it as a distinctive theme or thesis.

He would hold little interest for us if this positive conception of the relationship between the work and the author were entirely unproblematic, the mere strength of an example that, simply by being stated, could at once become effective. The poetic happiness that Binswanger considers to be the fulfillment of the self in art is for him (as for Bachelard with whom he has much in common), the most fragile form of happiness imaginable. For we were certainly misrepresenting his thought when we referred, a while ago, to this self-realization as an *expansion*. The sacrifices and renunciations that are demanded from the writer are not to be understood as a kind of bargain in which false values are being traded for safe ones. To the contrary, in the process the self is stripped of eminently concrete and legitimate attributes and is exposed at once to much more insidious forms of inauthenticity. Instead of speaking of *expansion* or fulfillment, Binswanger forces us to consider first of all the contraction, the reduction, that takes place in the subject as it engages in literary activity.

This reduction is paradoxical, for if we consider the question no longer from the point of view of the writer, but from that of the work he produces, we find nothing that resembles a reduction. The world created by the author and which can be called a "form" possesses attributes of fullness and totality. "Artistic productivity," writes Binswanger, "is the highest form of human productivity . . . because the form itself and only the form makes up the content of the productive action. The form constitutes the entity in its totality (die ganze Seinsphäre) and, as a result, it totally fulfills the modality of the aesthetic intention." "The work of art represents the total revelation of all entities in an artistic form that is necessarily liberating." [2]

In this context, the term "form" is not to be understood in a narrowly aesthetic sense, but as a project of fundamental totalization; in all these passages, the emphasis falls on the complete, fulfilled aspect of the work. But this totality of the form by no means implies a corresponding totality of the constitutive self. Neither in its origin, nor in its later development does the completeness of the form proceed from a fulfillment of the person who constitutes this form. The distinction between the personal self of the author and the self that reaches a measure of totality in the work becomes concretely manifest in these divergent destinies. The divergence is not a contingent accident but is constitutive of the work of art as such. Art originates in and by means of this divergence.

Binswanger finds a theoretical justification for the paradox that the plenitude of the work stems from a reduction of the self in an important, but perhaps not sufficiently known, article by Georg Lukács that dates back to 1917. The essay appeared in the journal *Logos* and is entitled "The Subject-Object Relationship in Aesthetics." Written in terminology that is primarily neo-Kantian and influenced by Rickert (the same Rickert who was one of Heidegger's teachers), the essay sets out to characterize the distinctive qualities of the aesthetic activity by distinguishing it from the structure of the logical and the ethical activities of the mind; the division corresponds to that of the three Kantian critiques. Without entering into the details of the analysis, we can limit ourselves to Lukács's conclusions about the relationship between the structure of the work and the subjectivity of the author. The structure is summarized in the description of the work as a "windowless monad" (eine fensterlose Monade), a concept that unites a notion of isolation with a notion of totality. On the one hand, the work is an entity that exists for and by itself, without any inherent possibility of entering into a relationship with other entities, even when these other entities are themselves aesthetic in kind. On the other hand, it is a cosmos; that is to say, perfectly self-sufficient within this isolation, since it can find within its own confines all

2. Ludwig Binswanger, *Hendrik Ibsen und das Problem der Selbstrealisation in der Kunst* (Heidelberg, 1949), pp. 21–22.

it needs for its existence and is in no way dependent on anything that would exist outside its boundaries. These boundaries, says Lukács, "are genuinely immanent, the kind of boundaries that only a cosmos can possess." [3] Even more important than the monadic structure of the work is the reason for its apparent immanence. It is not due to the objective nature of the aesthetic entity but, on the contrary, to the subjective intent that stands at the onset of its elaboration. The transcendental principle that determines the specificity of the work of art resides in the intent of the constitutive self to reduce itself to its own immanence, to eliminate everything that is not accessible to the immediate experience (Erlebbarkeit) of the self as self. The generality of the work of art is not a generality based on an act of reason—as in the case of a logical judgment—but based on the decision of a consciousness to clear itself of whatever, in consciousness, is not entirely immanent to it. "Contrary to the theoretical subject of logic," writes Lukács, "and contrary to the hypothetical subject of ethics, the stylized subject of aesthetics is a living unity that contains within itself the fullness of experience that makes up the totality of the human species." [4] But the only way in which this subject can succeed in remaining fully and exclusively consistent in its subjective nature is by concentrating on the elaboration of a fictional entity, by projecting itself into a form which although appearing to be autonomous and complete is actually determined by the subject itself. This fulfillment of the form clearly does not correspond to what one would consider, on the ethical or the practical level, as the harmonious development of a personality, the well-balanced development of faculties. Such a development would necessarily have to include objective factors of a physical, biological, social, and intersubjective nature that play no part in the autonomous world of aesthetics. The totalization is not a totalization in width but in depth, by means of which the subject resists any temptation of being distracted from its own self. Whereas the empirical self strives to take in as much as it can encompass and opens itself up to the presence of the world, the aesthetic self strives for a mode of

3. Georg Lukács, "Die Subjekt-Objekt Beziehung in der Ästhetik," *Logos* 1917–18, p. 19.
4. *Ibid.* p. 19.

totalization that is reductive but, in Lukács's term, "homogeneous" with its original intent at self-immanence.

For theoretical reasons, Lukács is led to consider what the monadic structure of the work implies for the self of the artist who produced it. His purpose in asking this question is not psychological, but appears in a discussion of the plurality inherent in any attempt to define the aesthetic entity. The work changes entirely with the point of view from which it is being examined, depending on whether one considers it as a finished form (*forma formata*) or, with the artist, as a form in the process of coming into being (*forma formans*). The problematic relationship between subject and object that prevails in the sphere of aesthetics is better understood when one considers it from the point of view of the author rather than from the point of view of the reader (or beholder). For the author is directly engaged in the ambiguities of aesthetic invention. As a free agent, his natural tendency would be to expand and to satisfy himself in the world-at-large, but he is constantly frustrated and curtailed by the restrictions that the form imposes upon him. Hence, in Lukács's words, "his isolation from all kinds and types of objective entities, from all forms . . . of human and collective relationships, as well as his isolation, as a subject, from all experiences not intended exclusively as the accomplishment of the work . . . his isolation, in short, from the entirety of his own personality." But, on the other hand, the artist knows that it is only by achieving the form that he can discover the objective correlative of the need for pure subjectivity that he carries within himself. Only in this way "can he reach the true and authentic subject-object relationship"—true and authentic as compared with the contrived relationship that exists in the field of logic or of ethics. He is therefore caught within a dilemma from which he can only escape by means of a Kierkegaardian leap: the work must become a project aimed toward an unreachable goal, and its partial success takes on the form of "a renunciation at the very moment when it comes into being." The work is a hyperbole in the Mallarméan sense, demanding that the subject forget itself in a projective act that can never coincide with its own desire. Expressing in a philosophical language a relationship between artist and work that resembles statements of Maurice Blanchot,

Lukács writes: "As the fulfillment of an artistic activity, the work is fully transcendental in relation to the constitutive subject. But the fact that it is . . . more than an object, although it is the only adequate objective expression of a subjectivity, is reflected in the infinite process of artistic activity and in the leap in which this activity culminates." [5]

This "solitary leap" of the poet—Mallarmé speaks, in a different but revealing context of death as a "solitaire bond"—reappears in the work of Binswanger in a more openly psychological form. Between Lukács's and Binswanger's text, however, intervenes a study by the phenomenologist Oskar Becker published in 1929 under the elaborate title: "Of the Fragility of the Beautiful and the Adventurous Nature of the Artist" ("Von der Hinfälligkeit des Schönen [the expression stems from Friedrich Solger's philosophical dialogue *Erwin*] und der Abenteuerlichkeit des Künstlers"). [6] In the time interval between the Lukács and the Becker essay, the publication of Heidegger's *Sein und Zeit* had taken place and Becker indeed interprets Lukács's conclusions in Heideggerian terms. The new self that results from Lukács's "homogeneous reduction" is now understood as a self capable of revealing the truth of its own destiny and of interpreting correctly its own mode of being. From the point of view of this "authentic" self, the distinction between author and reader—a distinction that was still momentarily maintained by Lukács—disappears. On the ontological level, reader and author are engaged in the same fundamental project and share an identical intent. The authentic reader —or critic—as well as the author now participate in the same perilous enterprise. This peril is described by Becker in terms of a new experience of temporality, as an attempt to exist in a time that would no longer be the fallen temporality of everyday existence. The artist projects himself into the future of his work as if it were possible to maintain an authentic temporality, but at the same time he knows this to be impossible, a pure *gageure*. He acts like an adventurer in entering upon a domain that he knows to lie beyond his reach. Becker characterizes the ambivalent status

5. *Ibid.* p. 35.
6. Oskar Becker, "Von der Hinfälligkeit des Schönen und der Abenteuerlichkeit des Künstlers" in *Festschrift für Edmund Husserl zum 70. Geburtstag* (1929).

of the aesthetic consciousness by the manner in which it fluctuates between two experiences of time: the temporality of everyday existence, that always falls back into estrangement and falsification, and another temporality that would remain clearly aware of its true mode of being. Becker's term for this mixed temporality is *Getragenheit,* "being carried." The artist is suspended as in the "rhythmique suspens du sinistre" that Mallarmé evokes by a succession of "suspended" sentences in *Un Coup de Dés,* carried aloft in the ambiguous time-structure of the monadic work.

Binswanger's own contribution consists in an interpretation of the "suspended" state of the artistic consciousness. He understands the urge to leap out of historical and everyday time first in negative terms, as it appears in the mood of harassment and oppression that torments a self imprisoned within its own facticity. A 1943 article has for its theme a quotation from Hugo von Hofmannsthal: "Was Geist ist, erfaszt nur der Bedrängte." [7] The term "der Bedrängte" is difficult to translate. It combines an idea of being locked up in too narrow a space, with the temporal ordeal of being steadily urged on, of being unable to remain at rest. One thinks of Pascal, of course, but also of man in Baudelaire, driven and harassed, "imitant la toupie et la boule":

> Singulière fortune où le but se déplace,
> Et, n'étant nulle part, peut être n'importe où!
> Où l'homme, dont jamais l'espérance n'est lasse
> Pour trouver le repos court toujours comme un fou!

Only the man who knows this feeling of harassed confinement, says Hofmansthal, can find access to the spirit, can aspire to the kind of tranquillity that exists nowhere but in the realm of the mind. Caught in this predicament, his first reaction will be the Baudelairian voyage into space, what Binswanger calls the "march into the distance," a search for new experiences to which one can find access without having to leave the horizontal expanse of the world. However, since the confinement is due not only to a lack of space, but is primarily caused by the excessive presence of time, these movements of horizontal expansion can never free the artist

7. Now in Ludwig Binswanger, *Ausgewählte Vorträge und Aufsätze,* Band II (Bern, 1955), pp. 243–52.

from his initial predicament. The failure of his quest for expansion
—which is indeed the theme of the Baudelaire poem "Le Voyage,"
as it is the theme of several essays by Binswanger—becomes clearly
apparent when it turns out that these horizontal displacements
are, in fact, devoid of danger. It is possible to lose one's way in the
distance, to be waylaid in the world of action to the point of
criminal transgression, but the kind of peril associated with the
fragility of the artist's mind can only occur when the *level* of existence undergoes a radical change. The transformation that allows
the artist to move from self-expansion and self-development to the
conquest of an altogether different kind of self is described by
Binswanger in terms of the metaphor of climbing and descending.
The phenomenology of distances, which befits the behavior of
the man of action, is replaced by a phenomenology of heights and
depths; the horizontal landscape of plain and sea becomes the
vertical landscape of the mountains.

The fragility of poetic transcendence, as compared with the relative safety of direct action, is represented by the anxieties associated with the feelings of height. The comings and goings of the
wanderer or the seafarer are voluntary and controlled actions but
the possibility of falling, which is forced upon the mountain
climber by an outside force, exists only in vertical space. The same
is true of experiences that are closely related to falling, such as
dizziness or relapses. This is another way of saying that, in the
experience of verticality, death is present in a more radical way
than in the experiences of the active life.

To the eventuality of the fall corresponds the possibility of an
equally involuntary ascent. It would seem at first sight that the
fall can only be oriented downwards, but Binswanger derives from
his own dream-theories the imaginative possibility of what could
be called an upward fall, and he finds a confirmation of his insight
in Gaston Bachelard's book *L'Air et les songes*. Bachelard and
Binswanger are referring to the feeling of being "carried away" by
an act of pure imagination, a feeling of levitation that is familiar
to readers of Keats and Wordsworth, for example. Poetic transcendence is closely akin to this act of spontaneous ascent, which
resembles an act of grace although it is only the manifestation of a
desire. As a result the subsequent "let-down," the possibility of

falling and of despondency that follows such moments of flight, is much more tragic and definitive than the mere fatigue of someone who climbs down, by his own devices, into the lower world of everyday cares.

There is still another danger that threatens the man willing to let himself be carried into the heights by the power of his own imagination: the danger of ascending beyond his own limits into a place from which he can no longer descend. Binswanger calls this condition a state of *Verstiegenheit,* a term that can be used in reference to a mountain-climber as well as to a symptom of mental pathology. The term plays an important part in Binswanger's psychiatric observations among the different types of false consciousness likely to lead to neuroses of the self. The man who, by his own vision, climbed above the limits of his own self and who is unable to return to earth without the assistance of others may well end up falling to his own destruction. According to Binswanger, artists are particularly susceptible to *Verstiegenheit* which, rather than hysteria or melancholy, appears as the pathological aspect of the poetic personality.

In trying to follow Binswanger's thought, we have been forced to introduce a terminology that derives from experimental psychology. Starting out from an ontological problem (the experience of the spatial structures of being) we have returned to problems of personality; in the last analysis Binswanger's concern seems to be aimed at the problems of the poetic personality rather than at the impersonal truth of the works. The reductive study of the self has led to the description of a specific type of false consciousness that is associated with the poetic temper; as a psychiatrist, Binswanger may feel called upon to reveal or even to cure this potential neurosis. This is not the intent of his more theoretical writings, however; for there can be no doubt that he consistently asserts the priority of literary over psychological concerns. Nevertheless, the organization of his essay on Ibsen suggests that, for him, the thematic content of a work of art must reveal the state of false consciousness to which the author has been brought by the very act of inventing the work. As a result, he chooses as an object for his inquiry a dramatist rather than a poet because the dramatist, Ibsen, has to stage more or less objectified states of false consciousness in conflict with each other, thus showing that he is able to under-stand and eventually to overcome these conflicts. And this is why, of all the plays by Ibsen, Binswanger prefers *The Master Builder,* which is precisely the story of a man who destroys himself be-cause he has, in a very literal way, built too tall a house on too shallow a foundation. The play is the perfect symbolical repre-sentation of *Verstiegenheit*. It therefore represents, for Binswanger, the clearest illustration of the self-mystification to which all artists, as artists, are bound to fall prey. This suffices for him to consider it Ibsen's masterpiece. He does not imply that Ibsen would have represented himself in the play in order to take shelter from dangers that threatened him while he was writing it. Binswanger is well aware of the mediations that separate the person from the work, and he never confuses poetic invention with therapy. But he sees the writer as necessarily reflecting the psychological dangers and satisfactions open to the transcendental self that is constituted both by and in the work of art.

This conclusion calls for some comment. It seems true enough that the destiny of a poetic consciousness is irrevocably bound up with the ontological "fall" that plays such a prominent part in Binswanger's thought and images. One could go so far as to say that the kind of knowledge contained in art is specifically the knowledge of this fall, the transformation of the experience of fall-ing into an act of knowledge. A certain degree of confusion arises when this knowledge is interpreted as a *means* to act upon the destiny that the knowledge reveals. This is the very moment at which the ontological inquiry is abandoned for empirical con-cerns that are bound to lead it astray. Binswanger's depth is best in evidence when he speaks of the initial anxiety of the poet as a harassed confinement, revealing his awareness of existence as a temporal predicament. Even as his description of the "fall," cap-tive of the pseudo-analogy implicit in his favorite spatial metaphor, gives a deceptive impression of concreteness, it remains less sub-stantial than in his predecessors: Lukács, Heidegger, and Becker. The upward fall is a highly suggestive way of designating the ambivalence that makes artistic invention into a paradoxical com-bination of free will and grace: he sees the imagination as an act of the individual will that remains determined, in its deepest in-

tent, by a transcendental moment that lies beyond our own vo-
lition; in this, he stays within the main tradition of the leading
theories of the imagination. But he fails to pursue the philosophical consequences of his insight and falls back upon a normative
precept favoring a harmonious relationship between extension and
depth as a necessary condition for a well-balanced personality. In
the last analysis, as a good psychiatrist, what interests Binswanger
most is the achievement of balance, not the truth of the fall.

Before we construe this as a criticism, we should remember how
difficult it is to remain rigorously confined to the disinterestedness
of non-empirical thought. Michel Foucault shows his awareness of
this difficulty when he criticizes phenomenology in the following
terms:

> Phenomenology, although it originated first of all in a climate
> of anti-psychologism . . . has never been able to free itself
> entirely from this insidious parenthood, from its tempting and
> threatening proximity to the empirical study of man. There-
> fore, although it starts out as a reduction to the *cogito,* it has
> always been led to ask questions, to ask the ontological ques-
> tion. We can see the phenomenological project dissolve under
> our very eyes into a description of actual experience that is
> empirical in spite of itself, and into an ontology of what lies
> beyond thought and thus bypasses the assumed primacy of
> the *cogito.*[8]

This could very well have been written with Binswanger in mind,
but it does not apply to either Husserl or Heidegger, both of whom
include this very danger among the constituents of their philosophical insight. Foucault himself owes his awareness of the problem to his grounding in phenomenology.

Some of the difficulties of contemporary criticism can be traced
back to a tendency to forsake the barren world of ontological reduction for the wealth of lived experience. Because it implies a
forgetting of the personal self for a transcendental type of self
that speaks in the work, the act of criticism can acquire exemplary
value. Although it is an asceticism of the mind rather than a
plenitude or a harmony, it is an asceticism that can lead to onto-

8. Michel Foucault, *op. cit.* p. 337.

logical insight. Contrary to Foucault's assertion, such an ontology can only bypass the primacy of the cogito if the "I" in the "I think" is conceived in too narrow a way. Literary criticism, in our century, has contributed to establishing this crucial distinction between an empirical and an ontological self; in that respect, it participates in some of the most audacious and advanced forms of contemporary thought.

IV

Georg Lukács's *Theory of the Novel*

The rather belated discovery of the work of Georg Lukács in the West and, most recently, in this country, has tended to solidify the notion of a very deep split between the early, non-Marxist and the later Marxist Lukács. It is certainly true that a sharp distinction in tone and purpose sets off such early essays as *Die Seele und die Formen* (1911) and *Die Theorie des Romans* (1914–15) from recently translated essays on literary subjects such as the *Studies in European Realism* (1953) or the political pamphlet *Wieder den mißverstandenen Realismus* (1957) published here under the title *Realism*. But the distinction can be overstated and misunderstood. It would be unsound, for instance, to hold on to the reassuring assumption that all the evil in the later Lukács came in as a result of his Marxist conversion; a considerable degree of continuity exists between a pre-Marxist work such as *Die Theorie des Romans* and the Marxist *Geschichte und Klassenbewußtsein*; it would be impossible for an admirer of the former to dismiss the latter entirely. There is a similar danger in an oversimplified view of a *good* early and a *bad* late Lukács. The works on realism have been treated very harshly on their American publication by such diverse critics as Harold Rosenberg (in *Dissent*) and Peter Demetz (in the *Yale Review*); on the other hand, *The Theory of the Novel* is being called by Harry Levin (*JHI,* January–March 1965, p. 150) "possibly the most penetrating essay that ever addressed itself to the elusive subject of the novel." If the blanket condemnation of the books on realism is clearly unjustified, especially if one bears in mind the considerable amount of debatable but interesting theoretical justification offered in Lukács's late *Ästhetik* (1963), the almost unqualified endorsement of *The Theory of the Novel* seems equally unwarranted. Whatever one may think of Lukács, he is certainly an important enough mind to be studied as a whole, and the critical interpretation of his thought has not been helped by the oversimplified division that has been established. The weaknesses of the later work are already present from the beginning, and some of the early strength remains operative throughout. Both weakness and strength, however, exist on a meaningful philosophical level and can only be understood in the larger perspective of nineteenth and twentieth-century intellectual history: they are part of the heritage of romantic and idealist thought. This stresses again the historical importance of Georg Lukács and rejects the frequent reproach made against him that he remains overconcerned with nineteenth-century modes of thought (a reproach that appears in both the Demetz and the Rosenberg reviews). Such criticism is inspired by an ill-conceived modernism or is made for propagandistic reasons.

I do not intend to address myself to the complex task of defining the unifying elements in Lukács's thought. By a brief critical examination of *The Theory of the Novel,* I hope to make some preliminary distinctions between what seems to remain valid and what has become problematic in this very concentrated and difficult essay. Written in a language that uses a pre-Hegelian terminology but a post-Nietzschean rhetoric, with a deliberate tendency to substitute general and abstract systems for concrete examples, *The Theory of the Novel* is by no means easy reading. One is particularly put off by the strange point of view that prevails throughout the essay: the book is written from the point of view of a mind that claims to have reached such an advanced degree of generality that it can speak, as it were, for the novelistic consciousness itself; it is the Novel itself that tells us the history of its own development, very much as, in Hegel's *Phenomenology*, it is the Spirit who narrates its own voyage. With this crucial difference, however, that since Hegel's Spirit has reached a full understanding of its own being, it can claim unchallengeable authority, a point which Lukács's novelistic consciousness, by its own avowal, is never allowed to reach. Being caught in its own contingency, and being indeed an expression of this contingency, it remains a mere phenomenon without regulative power; one would be led to expect a reductive, tentative and cautiously phenomenological approach rather than a sweeping history asserting its own laws. By translating the work in a less exalted language, one loses its moving and impressive philosophical pathos, but some of the preconceptions become more apparent.

Compared to a formalistic work such as, for instance, Wayne Booth's *Rhetoric of Fiction*, or to a work grounded in a more traditional view of history such as Auerbach's *Mimesis*, *The Theory of the Novel* makes much more radical claims. The emergence of the novel as the major modern genre is seen as the result of a change in the structure of human consciousness; the development of the novel reflects modifications in man's way of defining himself in relation to all categories of existence. Lukács is not offering us, in this essay, a sociological theory that would explore relationships between the structure and development of the novel and those of society, nor is he proposing a psychological theory explaining the novel in terms of human relationships. Least of all do we find him conferring an autonomy on formal categories that would give them a life of their own, independently of the more general intent that produces them. He goes instead to the most general possible level of experience, a level on which the use of terms such as Destiny, the Gods, Being, etc. seems altogether natural. The vocabulary and the historical scheme is that of later eighteenth-century aesthetic speculation; one is indeed constantly reminded of Schiller's philosophical writings on reading Lukács's formulation of the distinctions between the main literary genres.

The distinction between the epic and the novel is founded on a distinction between the Hellenic and the Western mind. As in

Schiller, this distinction is stated in terms of the category of alienation, seen as an intrinsic characteristic of the reflective consciousness. Lukács's description of alienation is eloquent, but not strikingly original; the same could be said of his corresponding description at the beginning of the essay of a harmonious unity in the
ideal Greece. The original unified nature that surrounds us in
"the blessed times . . . when the fire that burns in our souls is
of the same substance as the fire of the stars" [1] has now been split
in fragments that are "nothing but the historical form of the alienation (Entfremdung) between man and his works (seine Gebil-
den)." And the following text could take its place among the great
elegiac quotations of the early nineteenth century: "The epic individual, the hero of the novel, originates in the alienation from
the outside world. As long as the world is inwardly one, no real
qualitative distinctions occur among its inhabitants; they may well
be heroes and scoundrels, worthy men and criminals, but the greatest hero only rises by a head's length above his fellow-men, and
the noble words of the wise can be understood even by the fools.
The autonomy of inwardness becomes possible and necessary only
when the differences between men have grown to be an unbreach-
able gap; when the gods have grown silent and no sacrifice or prayer
is capable of loosening their tongues; when the world of action
loses contact with that of the self, leaving man empty and powerless, unable to grasp the real meaning of his deeds . . . : when
inwardness and adventure are forever distinct." We are much
closer here to Schiller than to Marx.

A definitely post-Hegelian element is introduced with Lukács's
insistence on the need for totality as the inner necessity that shapes
all works of art. The unity of the Hellenic experience of the world
has a formal correlative in the creation of closed, *total* forms, and
this desire for totality is an inherent need of the human mind. It
persists in modern, alienated man, but instead of fulfilling itself in
the mere expression of his given unity with the world, it becomes
instead the statement of an intent to retrieve the unity it no
longer possesses. Clearly, Lukács's idealized fiction of Greece is a
device to state a theory of consciousness that has the structure of

1. All quotations from *Die Theorie des Romans,* Zweite Auflage, Berlin, 1963.
The first edition is from 1920.

an intentional movement. This implies, in turn, a presupposition about the nature of historical time, to which we will have to return later.

Lukács's theory of the novel emerges in a cogent and coherent way out of the dialectic between the urge for totality and man's alienated situation. The novel becomes "the epic of a world from which God has departed" (p. 87). As a result of the separation between our actual experience and our desire, any attempt at a total understanding of our being will stand in contrast to actual experience, which is bound to remain fragmentary, particular and unfulfilled. This separation between life (Leben) and being (Wesen) is reflected historically in the decline of the drama and the parallel rise of the novel. For Lukács, the drama is the medium in which, as in Greek tragedy, the most universal predicament of man is to be represented. At a moment in history in which such universality is absent from all actual experiences, the drama has to separate itself entirely from life, to become ideal and otherworldly; the German classical theater after Lessing serves Lukács as an example for this retreat. The novel, to the contrary, wishing to avoid this most destructive type of fragmentation remains rooted instead in the particularlity of experience; as an epical genre, it can never give up its contact with empirical reality, which is an inherent part of its own form. But, in a time of alienation, it is forced to represent this reality as imperfect, as steadily striving to move beyond the boundaries that restrict it, as constantly experiencing and resenting the inadequacy of its own size and shape. "In the novel, what is constituted is not the totality of life but rather the relationship, the valid or mistaken position of the writer who enters the scene as an empirical subject in his full stature, but also in his full limitation as a mere creature, towards this totality." The theme of the novel is thus necessarily limited to the individual, and to this individual's frustrating experience of his own inability to acquire universal dimensions. The novel originates in the Quixotic tension between the world of romance and that of reality. The roots of Lukács's later dogmatic commitment to realism are certainly to be found in this aspect of his theory. However, at the time of *The Theory of the Novel*, the insistence on the necessary presence of an empirical element in the novel is altogether convincing, all the

more so since it is counterbalanced by the attempt to overcome
the limitations of reality.

This thematic duality, the tension between an earth-bound destiny and a consciousness that tries to transcend this condition,
leads to structural discontinuities in the form of the novel. Totality
strives for a continuity that can be compared with the unity of an
organic entity, but the estranged reality intrudes upon this continuity and disrupts it. Next to a "homogeneous and organic stability" the novel also displays a "heterogeneous and contingent discontinuity" (p. 74). This discontinuity is defined by Lukács as
irony. The ironic structure acts disruptively, yet it reveals the
truth of the paradoxical predicament that the novel represents.
For this reason, Lukács can state that irony actually provides the
means by which the novelist transcends, within the form of the
work, the avowed contingency of his condition. "In the novel,
irony is the freedom of the poet in relation to the divine . . . for
it is by means of irony that, in an intuitively ambiguous vision, we
can perceive divine presence in a world forsaken by the gods."
This concept of irony as the positive power of an absence also stems
directly from Lukács's idealist and romantic ancestors; it reveals the
influence of Friedrich Schlegel, of Hegel and most of all of Hegel's
contemporary Solger. Lukács's originality resides in his use of
irony as a structural category.

For if irony is indeed the determining and organizing principle
of the novel's form, then Lukács is indeed freeing himself from
preconceived notions about the novel as an imitation of reality.
Irony steadily undermines this claim at imitation and substitutes
for it a conscious, interpreted awareness of the distance that separates an actual experience from the understanding of this experience. The ironic language of the novel mediates between experience and desire, and unites ideal and real within the complex paradox of the form. This form can have nothing in common with the
homogeneous, organic form of nature: it is founded on an act of
consciousness, not on the imitation of a natural object. In the novel
". . . the relationship of the parts to the whole, although it tries
to come as close as possible to being an organic relationship, is in
fact an ever-suspended *conceptual* relationship, not a truly organic
one" (p. 74). Lukács comes very close, in statements of this kind,

to reaching a point from which a genuine hermeneutic of the novel could start.

His own analysis, however, seems to move in a different direction; the second part of the essay contains a sharp critical rejection of the kind of inwardness that is associated with a hermeneutic theory of language. In the 1961 preface which Lukács added to the recent reissue of his essay, he scornfully refers to the phenomenological approach as a "right-wing epistemology," that runs counter to the left-wing ethics. This criticism was already implicit in the original text. When he comes closest to dealing with contemporary developments in the novel and with moments in which the novel itself seems to become conscious of its real intent, a revealing shift in the argument takes place. He shows us, convincingly enough, how inwardness for its own sake can lead to an evasion of the novel into a falsely Utopian realm "a Utopia which, from the start, has a bad conscience and a knowledge of its own defeat" (p. 119). The romantic novel of disillusion (Desillusionsromantik) is the example of this distortion of the genre, in which the novel loses contact with empirical reality; Lukács is thinking of Novalis, who was attacked in similar terms in an essay from the earlier book *Die Seele und die Formen,* but he also gives examples from Jacobsen's *Niels Lyhne* and Gontcharov's *Oblomov.* He fully realizes, however, that these examples do not account for other developments in European fiction in which the same theme of disillusion is obviously present and which he neither can nor wishes to dismiss. Flaubert's *Sentimental Education,* of course, is the most striking instance, a truly modern novel shaped by the overpowering negativity of an almost obsessive inwardness but which nevertheless, in Lukács's own judgment, represents the highest achievement of the genre in the nineteenth century. What is present in Flaubert's *Sentimental Education* that saves it from being condemned together with other post-romantic novels of inwardness?

At this moment in the argument, Lukács introduces an element that had not been explicitly mentioned up till now: temporality. In the 1961 Preface, he points with pride to the original use of the category of time, at a moment when Proust's novel was not yet known to the public. For the decadent and belated romantic, time is experienced as pure negativity; the inward action of the novel is a hopeless "battle against the erosive power of time." But in Flaubert, according to Lukács, this is precisely not the case. In spite of the hero's continuous defeats and disappointments, time triumphs as a positive principle in the *Sentimental Education,* because Flaubert succeeds in recapturing the irresistible feeling of flow that characterizes Bergsonian *durée.* "It is time which makes possible this victory. The uninterrupted and irrepressible flow of time is the unifying principle that gives homogeneity to the disjointed parts, by putting them in a relationship that, although irrational and ineffable, is nevertheless one of unity. Time gives order to the random agitation of men and confers upon it the appearance of organic growth . . ." (p. 128). On the level of true temporal experience, the ironic discontinuities vanish and the treatment of time itself, in Flaubert, is no longer ironic.

Can we admit Lukács's interpretation of the temporal structure of the *Sentimental Education?* When Proust, in a polemical exchange with Thibaudet, discussed Flaubert's style in terms of temporality, what he emphasized was not homogeneity but precisely the opposite: the manner in which Flaubert's use of tenses allowed him to create discontinuities, periods of dead and negative time alternating with moments of pure origination, complexities in memory structures comparable to those achieved by Gérard de Nerval in *Sylvie.* The single-directed flow of mere *durée* is replaced by a complex juxtaposition of reversible movements that reveal the discontinuous and polyrhythmic nature of temporality. But such a disclosure of non-linear temporality demands reductive moments of inwardness in which a consciousness confronts its own true self; and this moment is precisely the one at which the organic analogy between subject and object reveals itself as false.

It seems that the organicism which Lukács had eliminated from the novel when he made irony its guiding structural principle, has reentered the picture in the guise of time. Time in this essay acts as a substitute for the organic continuity which Lukács seems unable to do without. Such a linear conception of time had in fact been present throughout the essay. Hence the necessity of narrating the development of the novel as a continuous event, as the fallen form of the archetypal Greek epic which is treated as an ideal concept but given actual historical existence. The later development of Lukács's theories on the novel, the retreat from Flaubert back to Balzac, from Dostoevsky to a rather simplified view of Tolstoi, from a theory of art as interpretation to a theory of art as reflected imitation (Wiederspiegelung) should be traced back to the reified idea of temporality that is so clearly in evidence at the end of *Theory of the Novel.*

V

Impersonality in the Criticism of Maurice Blanchot

Since the end of the war, French literature has been dominated by a succession of quickly alternating intellectual fashions that have kept alive the illusion of a fecund and productive modernity. First came the vogue of Sartre, Camus, and the humanistic existentialism that followed immediately in the wake of the war, soon to be succeeded by the experimentalism of the new theater, bypassed in turn by the advent of the *nouveau roman* and its epigones. These movements are, to a large extent, superficial and ephemeral; the traces they will leave on the history of French literature is bound to be slighter than it appears within the necessarily limited perspective of our own contemporaneity. Not all the more significant literary figures necessarily remained aloof from these trends; several took part in them and were influenced by them. But the true quality of their literary vocation can be tested by the persistence with which they kept intact a more essential part of themselves, a part that remained untouched by the vicissitudes of a literary production oriented toward public recognition—arcane and esoteric as this "public" may have been.

For some, like Sartre, this self-assertion took the form of a frantic attempt to maintain a firm inner commitment in open and polemical contact with the changing trends. But others kept themselves more consciously out of the reach of the surface-currents and were carried by a slower and deeper wave, closer to the continuities that link French writing of today to its past. When we will be able to observe the period with more detachment, the main proponents of contemporary French literature may well turn out to be figures that now seem shadowy in comparison with the celebrities of the hour. And none is more likely to achieve future prominence than the little-publicized and difficult writer, Maurice Blanchot.

Even the fashionable trends to which we alluded are characterized by a constant intermingling of literary practice and critical theory. Sartre and his group were the theoretical exponents of their own stylistic devices, and the affinities between structuralist criticism and the *nouveau roman* are obvious. In Blanchot, the same interplay occurs, in a more complex and problematic way, between his work as a writer of narrative prose and his critical essays. An intensely private figure, who has kept his personal affairs strictly to himself and whose pronouncements on public issues, literary or political, have been very scarce, Blanchot is primarily known as a critic. A sizable group of readers have followed his essays, often appearing in the form of topical book-reviews in various journals none of which is particularly esoteric or avant-garde: *Journal des débats, Critique,* and more recently in *La Nouvelle revue française* to which Blanchot used to contribute a monthly article. These essays have been gathered in volumes (*Faux-pas,* 1943, *La Part du feu,* 1949, *L'Espace littéraire,* 1955, *Le Livre à venir,* 1959) that bring out Blanchot's almost obsessive preoccupation with a few fundamental concerns, thus reducing their apparent diversity to an implacably repetitive uniformity. The influence of the critical work has been far-reaching. More philosophical and abstract than Charles du Bos and less conducive to practical application than Bachelard's theories of material imagery, Blanchot's criticism has remained aloof from recent methodological debates and polemics. Yet his already considerable impact is bound to increase; rather than directly affecting

existing critical methods, his work puts into question the very
conditions prior to the elaboration of all critical discourse and in
that way reaches a level of awareness no other contemporary
critic has reached.

It is clear that Blanchot derives much of his insight into the
work of others from his own experience as a writer of narrative
prose.[1] Until now, his novels and *récits* have remained nearly
inaccessible in their labyrinthine obscurity. All that has to be
said about them, in an article dealing with the critical work, is
that it is fortunately a great deal easier to gain access to the
fiction of Blanchot through his criticism than the other way
round. The crux of the interpretation of this writer, one of the
most important of the century, lies no doubt in a clarification of
the relationship between the critical and the narrative part of his
work. A description of the movement of his critical mind is a valid
preliminary to such an inquiry.

Reading Maurice Blanchot differs from all other reading experiences. One begins by being seduced by the limpidity of a
language that allows for no discontinuities or inconsistencies.
Blanchot is, in a way, the clearest, the most lucid of writers: he
steadily borders on the inexpressible and approaches the extreme
of ambiguity, but always recognizes them for what they are; consequently, as in Kant, the horizon of our understanding remains
clearly circumscribed. When we read him on one of the poets
or novelists he happens to choose for a theme, we readily forget
all we assumed to know up till then about this writer. This does
not happen because Blanchot's insight necessarily compels us to
modify our own perspective; this is by no means always the case.
Returning afterwards to the author in question, we will find
ourselves back at the same point, our understanding barely enriched by the comments of the critic. Blanchot, in fact, never
intended to perform a task of exegesis that would combine earlier
acquired knowledge with new elucidations. The clarity of his

1. Some of these fictions are called novels, such as, among others, *Thomas
l'obscur* (1941), *Aminadab* (1942), *Le Très-haut* (1948); while others are
called *récits*: *Thomas l'obscur*, new version (1950), *Au Moment voulu* (1951),
Celui qui ne m'accompagnait pas (1953).

critical writings is not due to exegetic power; they seem clear, not because they penetrate further into a dark and inaccessible domain but because they suspend the very act of comprehension. The light they cast on texts is of a different nature. Nothing, in fact, could be more obscure than the nature of this light.

For how are we to understand a reading-process which, in Blanchot's words, is located "au delà ou en deçà de la compréhension" before or beyond the act of understanding? (*L'Espace littéraire*, p. 205.) The difficulty of defining this conception indicates how much it differs from our ordinary assumptions about criticism. Blanchot's critical reflections offer us no personal confessions or intimate experiences, nothing that would give immediate access to another person's consciousness and allow the reader to espouse its movements. A certain degree of inwardness prevails in his work and makes it into the very opposite of an objective narrative. But this intimacy does not seem to belong to a particularized self, for his prose reveals nothing about his private experience. The language is as little a language of self-confession as it is a language of exegesis. And, even in the articles that are obviously inspired by topical literary considerations, it is least of all a language of evaluation or of opinion. In reading Blanchot, we are not participating in an act of judgment, of sympathy, or of understanding. As a result, the fascination we experience is accompanied by a feeling of resistance, by a refusal to be led to a confrontation with something opaque on which our consciousness can find no hold. The ambivalence of this experience can be somewhat clarified by Blanchot's own statements.

> The act of reading does not change anything, nor does it add anything to what was already there; it lets things be the way they were; it is a form of freedom, not the freedom that gives or takes away, but a freedom that accepts and consents, that says yes. It can only say yes, and, in the space opened up by this affirmation, it allows the work to assert itself as the unsettling decision of its will to be—and nothing more.[2]

At first sight this passive and silent encounter with the work seems to be the very opposite of what we usually call interpretation. It

2. *L'Espace littéraire* (Paris, 1955), p. 202.

differs entirely from the subject-object polarities involved in objective observation. The literary work is given no objective status whatever; it has no existence apart from that constituted by the inward act of reading. Neither are we dealing with a so-called intersubjective or interpersonal act, in which two subjects engage in a self-clarifying dialogue. It would be more accurate to say that the two subjectivities involved, that of the author and that of the reader, co-operate in making each other forget their distinctive identity and destroy each other as subjects. Both move beyond their respective particularity toward a common ground that contains both of them, united by the impulse that makes them turn away from their particular selves. It is by means of the act of reading that this turning away takes place; for the author, the possibility of being read transforms his language from a mere project into a work (and thus forever detaches it from him). In turn, it brings the reader back, for a moment, to what he might have been before he shaped himself into a particular self.

This conception of reading seems to differ altogether from interpretation. "It adds nothing to what was already there," says Blanchot; whereas it seems to be of the essence of interpretation to generate a language at the contact of another language, to be a kind of over-language added to that of the work. But we must not be misled by concepts of interpretation that derive from objective and intersubjective models. Blanchot expects us to understand the act of reading in terms of the work and not in terms of the constitutive subject, although he carefully avoids giving the work an objective status. He wants us "to take the work for what it is and thus to rid it of the presence of the author . . ." (*L'Espace littéraire*, p. 202). What we are reading is located closer to its origin than we are and it is our purpose to be attracted by it to the place whence it issued. The work has an undeniable ontological priority over the reader. It follows that it would be absurd to claim that in reading we "add" something, for any addition, be it in the form of an explication, a judgment, or an opinion, will only remove us further from the real center. We can only come under the true spell of the work by allowing it to remain what it is. This apparently passive act, this "nothing" that, in reading, we should *not* add to the work, is the very definition of a truly interpretative language. It designates a positive way of addressing the text, noticeable in the positive emphasis that characterizes the description of the act of reading, a rare example of affirmation in an author not prone to positive statement. The urge to let a work be exactly what it is requires an active and unrelenting vigilance, which can only be exercised by means of language. In this manner, an interpretative language originates in contact with the work. To the extent that reading merely "listens" to the work, it becomes itself an act of interpretative understanding.[3] Blanchot's description of the act of reading defines authentic interpretation. In depth, it transcends descriptions of interpretation that derive from the study of things or from the analysis of individual subjects.

Yet, Blanchot feels the need to qualify his definition by an all-important reservation. The act of reading, by means of which the authentic dimensions of a work can be revealed, can never be performed by the author on his own writings. Blanchot frequently states this impossibility perhaps most clearly at the beginning of *L'Espace littéraire*:

> . . . the writer can never read his own work. It is, for him, strictly inaccessible, a secret which he does not wish to confront. . . . The impossibility of self-reading coincides with the discovery that, from now on, there is no longer room for any added creation in the space opened up by the work and that, consequently, the only possibility is that of forever writing the same work over again. . . . The particular loneliness of the writer . . . stems from the fact that, in the work, he belongs to what always precedes the work.[4]

The statement is of central importance for an understanding of Blanchot. At first sight, it seems convincing enough: we can find many examples, in the course of literary history, of the estrangement experienced by writers who handle their language seriously, when they face the expression of their own thought, and Blanchot links this estrangement with the difficulty of renouncing the belief that all literature is a new beginning, that a work is a sequence of beginnings. We may believe that the greater proximity to origin

3. Cf. Martin Heidegger, "Logos" in *Vorträge und Aufsätze* (Neske: Pfullingen, 1954), pp. 215 ff.
4. *L'Espace littéraire*, p. 14; see also p. 209.

confers upon the work some of the "firmness of beginnings" that Blanchot is willing to grant to the work of others. But this strength is only an illusion. The poet can only start his work because he is willing to forget that this presumed beginning is, in fact, the repetition of a previous failure, resulting precisely from an inability to begin anew. When we think that we are perceiving the assertion of a new origin, we are in fact witnessing the reassertion of a failure to originate. Acceding to the work in its positivity, the reader can very well ignore what the author was forced to forget: that the work asserted in fact the impossibility of its own existence. However, if the writer were really reading himself, in the full interpretative sense of the term, he would necessarily remember the duplicity of his self-induced forgetfulness, and this discovery would paralyze all further attempts at creation. In that sense, Blanchot's *noli me legere*, the rejection of self-interpretation, is an expression of caution, advocating a prudence without which literature might be threatened with extinction.

The impossibility of a writer's reading his own work sharply distinguishes the relationship between work and reader from that between work and author. Reading, as well as criticism (conceived as the actualization in language of the potential language involved in reading), can grow into a genuine interpretation, in the deepest sense of the term, whereas the relationship between author and work would be one of total estrangement, refusal, and forgetting. This radical distinction raises several questions. It seems primarily motivated by caution, a virtue that is not typical of the almost ruthless audacity of Blanchot's thought. Moreover, the study of Blanchot's later work reveals that the process of forgetting, itself deeply linked with the impossibility of the author's reading his own work, is, in fact, a much more ambiguous matter than may have appeared at first sight. The positive assertion of the work is not merely the result of a complicity between reader and author that enables the one to ignore what the other is willing to forget. The will to forget enables the work to exist and becomes a positive notion leading to the invention of an authentic language. Blanchot's recent work compels us to become aware of the full ambivalence of the power contained in the act of forgetting. It reveals the paradoxical presence of a kind of anti-memory at the very source of literary creation. If this is so, can we still believe that Blanchot refuses to read his work and dodges confrontation with his literary self? The remembrance of a forgetting can occur only while reading the work, not in the course of its composition. The reading that allows Blanchot to move from the first to the second version of his early novel *Thomas l'obscur* could still be explained as an attempt "to repeat what was said earlier . . . with the power of an increased talent." But the dialogue of the late text entitled, *L'Attente l'oubli* could only be the result of a relationship between the completed work and its author. The impossibility of self-reading has itself become the main theme, demanding in its turn to be read and interpreted. A circular movement seems to take the writer, at first alienated in the work, back to himself, by means of an act of self-interpretation. In Blanchot, this process first takes the form of his critical reading of others as preparatory to the reading of himself. It can be shown that Blanchot's criticism prefigures the self-reading toward which he is ultimately oriented. The relationship between his critical work and his narrative prose has to be understood in these terms, the former being the preparatory version of the latter. A complete study of Blanchot should illustrate this by means of several examples; we have space for one instance only, the sequence of articles he wrote on Mallarmé. This may suffice to indicate that the movement of Blanchot's critical mind reflects the circular pattern that can be found in all acts of literary invention.

Mallarmé is one of the writers who have constantly engaged Blanchot's attention; the poet of *Un Coup de Dés* reappears as one of his main topics at all stages of his development. Since Blanchot writes in the traditional French format of the periodical review, his choice of subject-matter is not always dictated by a deeper affinity with the book he criticizes; it may be inspired by current fashion or by the pressure of literary events. In accordance with his conception of criticism, he is not interested in the discovery of new talent or in the revaluation of established names. In his selection of topics, he is generally content to follow a cosmopolitan current of opinion that is well informed but lays no claim to originality. There are, however, a few figures that recur as the true centers of his concern. Mallarmé is undoubtedly one of them; the identity of the other writers that influenced Blanchot may often remain hidden, but Mallarmé is explicitly discussed on various occasions.

Above all, Mallarmé fascinates Blanchot by his claim to absolute impersonality. The other main themes of Mallarmé's work, the large negative themes of death, ennui, and sterility, or even the self-reflection by which literature "scrutinizes its very essence," all take second place to the *gageure* of letting the work exist only by and for itself. Blanchot frequently quotes the statement of Mallarmé which he considers of central importance: "Impersonifié, le volume, autant qu'on s'en sépare comme auteur, ne réclame approche de lecteur. Tel, sache, entre les accessoires humains, il a lieu tout seul: fait, étant." [5] Impersonality means, in the first place, the absence of all personal anecdotes, of all confessional intimacies, and of all psychological concerns. Mallarmé eschews such forms of experience, not because he considers them as devoid of importance, but because the generality of poetic language has moved far beyond them. Hence the naïveté of reductive critical methods that try to gain access to Mallarmé's poetry by tracing it back to actual private experiences. One is never so far removed from the center as when one assumes to have recaptured the origin of the self in an empirical experience that is taken to be the cause. Blanchot is not likely to be misled in this direction: his negative comments on Charles Mauron's first psychoanalytical study of Mallarmé, dating as far back as 1943, are still altogether valid and topical.

Mallarmé's impersonality cannot be described as the antithesis, or the compensatory idealization, of a regressive obsession, as a strategy by means of which the poet tries to free himself from haunting emotional or sexual trauma. We do not find in him a dialectic of the empirical and the ideal self, as Freud describes it in the Narcissus essay. More than all other critics who have written on Mallarmé, Blanchot stressed most emphatically, from the start, that the impersonality of Mallarmé does not result from a conflict

5. "The book when we, as authors, separate ourselves from it, exists impersonally, without requiring the presence of a reader. Know that, among all human accessories, it is the one that comes into being by itself; it is made, and exists, by itself." (*L'Action restreinte, Oeuvres complètes* [Paris, 1945], p. 372.)

within his own person. It stems instead from a confrontation with an entity as different from himself as non-being differs from being. Mallarmé's alienation is neither social nor psychological, but ontological; to be impersonal does not mean, for him, that one shares a consciousness or a destiny with a number of others, but that one is reduced to no longer being a person, to being no one, because one defines onself in relation to being and not in relation to some particular entity.

In an article that dates back to 1949, Blanchot stresses that, for Mallarmé, the only medium by means of which such impersonality can be achieved is language. "Many striking points [about Mallarmé's conception of language] are to be remembered. The most remarkable, however, is the impersonality of language, the autonomous and absolute existence Mallarmé is willing to grant it. . . . Language supposes for him neither a speaker, nor a listener: it speaks and writes by itself. It is a kind of consciousness without a subject." [6] The poet thus encounters language as an alien and self-sufficient entity, not at all as if it were the expression of a subjective intent with which he could grow familiar, still less a tool that could be made to fit his needs. Yet it is well known that Mallarmé always used language in the manner of the Parnassian poets, the way a craftsman uses the material in which he is working. Well aware of this, Blanchot adds: "But language is also an incarnate consciousness that has been seduced into taking on the material form of words, their life and their sound, and leading one to believe that this reality can somehow open up a road that takes one to the dark center of things." [7] This important qualification leads us at once to the heart of the Mallarméan dialectic. For it is true that Mallarmé always conceived of language as a separate entity radically different from himself, and which he was incessantly trying to reach; the model for this entity, however, was mostly for him the mode of being of a natural substance, accessible to sensation. Language, with its sensory attributes of sound and texture, partakes of the world of natural objects and introduces a positive element in the sheer void that would surround a consciousness left entirely to itself. The double aspect of language, capable —

6. *La Part du feu* (Paris, 1949), p. 48.
7. *La Part du feu,* p. 48.

of being at the same time a concrete, natural thing and the product of an activity of consciousness, serves Mallarmé as the starting point of a dialectical development that runs through his entire work. Nature, far from representing the satisfaction of a happy, unproblematic sensation, evokes instead separation and distance; nature is for him the substance from which we are forever separated. But it is also "La première en date, la nature" and, as such, it precedes all other entities and occupies a privileged position of priority. This assumption is of determining importance for the genesis and the structure of Mallarmé's work. The symbols of failure and of negativity that play such an important role in his poetry must be understood in terms of the underlying polarity between the world of nature and the activity of consciousness. Reacting against the natural world in an attempt to assert his autonomy, the poet discovers that he can never free himself from its impact. The final image of Mallarmé's work shows the protagonist of *Un Coup de Dés* sinking into the "ocean" of the natural world. Nevertheless, in a gesture that is both heroic and absurd, the will to consciousness keeps asserting itself, even from beyond the catastrophic event in which it was destroyed. The persistence of this effort keeps carrying the work forward and engenders a trajectory that seems to escape, to some extent, from the chaos of indetermination. This trajectory is reflected in the very structure of Mallarmé's development and constitutes the positive element that allows him to pursue his task. The work consists of a sequence of new beginnings that are not, however, as for Blanchot, identical repetitions. The eternal repetition, the *ressassement* of Blanchot is replaced, in Mallarmé, by a dialectical movement of becoming. Each successive failure knows and remembers the failure that went before, and this knowledge establishes a progression. Mallarmé's self-reflection is rooted in experiences that are not altogether negative, but that nevertheless maintain a certain measure of self-awareness, "la clarté reconue, qui seule demeure. . . ." [8] Subsequent work can start on a higher level of consciousness than their predecessors. There is room in Mallarmé's world for some form of memory; from work to work, one is not allowed to forget

8. ". . . a recognized clarity, the only thing to remain" (*Igitur, Oeuvres complètes*, p. 435).

what went before. A link is maintained, despite the discontinuities, and a movement of growth takes place. The impersonality is the result of a dialectical progression, leading from the particular to the universal, from personal to historical recollection. The work depends for its existence on this dialectical substructure, which is itself rooted in an obscure assertion of the priority of material substances over consciousness. Mallarmé's poetics remain founded on the attempt to make the semantic dimensions of language coincide with its material, formal attributes.[9]

Such an attempt should not be confused with Blanchot's experiments. When Blanchot speaks, in the passage previously quoted, of language as an "incarnate consciousness" (adding at once that this may well be a delusion), he is describing a conception of language that differs altogether from his own. Blanchot's writing very seldom lingers over the material qualities of things; without being abstract, his language is rarely a language of sensation. His preferred literary form is not, as for René Char with whom he is often compared, that of a poetry oriented toward material things, but rather the récit, a purely temporal type of narrative. It should not surprise us, therefore, that his presentation of Mallarmé at times misses the mark. This is particularly true of the sections of L'Espace littéraire in which Blanchot deals with the theme of death as it appears in Mallarmé's prose text Igitur. However, when Blanchot returns to Mallarmé later, in the articles now included in Le Livre à venir, his observations lead to a general view that is a genuine interpretation.

What is missing, perhaps deliberately, in Blanchot's commentaries on Igitur, is precisely this sense of dialectical growth by

9. Recent interpreters of Mallarmé, such as Jacques Derrida and Philippe Sollers, anticipated in some respects by the American critic Robert Greer Cohn, find in Mallarmé a movement that takes place within the textual aspect of language as mere signifier, regardless of a natural or subjective referent. As is clear from the spatial, representational interpretation of the ideograms of Un Coup de Dés (as in the passages quoted below and identified by footnotes 11 and 12), Blanchot's reading of Mallarmé never reaches this point. He remains within a negative subject/object dialectic in which an impersonal non-subject confronts an abolished non-object ("rien" or "l'absente"). This layer of meaning is undoubtedly present in Mallarmé and we can remain within the orbit of this understanding for an argument that deals with Blanchot (or, more restrictively, with Blanchot's critical assumptions) and not with Mallarmé.

means of which the particular death of the protagonist becomes
a universal movement, corresponding to the historical development
of human consciousness in time. Blanchot translates the experience
at once in ontological terms and sees it as a direct confrontation
of a consciousness with the most general category of being. Igitur's
death then becomes for him a version of one of his own main
obsessions, what he calls "la mort impossible," a theme more
closely affiliated with Rilke and one that does not fully coincide
with Mallarmé's chief concern at the time of *Igitur*. The distortion is in keeping with Blanchot's deeper commitments: Mallarmé's theme of the universal historical consciousness, with its
Hegelian overtones, is of slight interest to him. He considers the
dialectic of subject and object, the progressive temporality of a
historical growth, as inauthentic experiences, misleading reflections
of a more fundamental movement that resides in the realm of
being. Later, when Mallarmé will have pursued his own thought
to its most extreme point, he will at last convey the oscillatory
movement within being that Blanchot prematurely claims to
find stated in *Igitur*. It is at this point that a real encounter between
Blanchot and Mallarmé can take place.

Blanchot's final interpretation of Mallarmé occurs in the essays
from *Le Livre à venir* that deal with *Un Coup de Dés* and with
the preparatory notes which Jacques Scherer edited in 1957 under
the title *Le "Livre" de Mallarmé*. In *Hérodiade, Igitur,* and the
poems that follow these texts, Mallarmé's main theme had been
the destruction of the object under the impact of a reflective consciousness, the near dissolution ("la presque disparition vibra-
toire") of natural entities and of the self, raised to an advanced
level of impersonality when, in the mirror of self-reflection, it
becomes the object of its own thought. But in the process of depersonalization, the self could, to some degree, maintain its power;
enriched by the repeated experience of defeat, it remained as the
center of work, the point of departure of the spiral that grows out
of it. Later on, in *Un Coup de Dés*, the dissolution of the object
occurs on such a large scale that the entire cosmos is reduced to
total indetermination; "la neutralité identique du gouffre," an abyss
in which all things are equal in their utter indifference to the
human mind and will. This time, however, the conscious self par-

ticipates in the process to the point of annihilation: "The poet," writes Blanchot, "disappears under the pressure of the work, caught in the same movement that prompted the disappearance of the reality of nature." [10] Pushed to this extreme point, the impersonality of the self is such that it seems to lose touch with its initial center and to dissolve into nothingness. It now becomes clear that dialectical growth toward a universal consciousness was a delusion and that the notion of a progressive temporality is a reassuring but misleading myth. In truth, consciousness was caught unawares within a movement that transcends its own power. The various forms of negation that had been "surmounted" as the work progressed—death of the natural object, death of the individual consciousness in *Igitur*, or the destruction of a universal, historical consciousness destroyed in the "storm" of *Un Coup de Dés* —turn out to be particular expressions of a persistent negative movement that resides in being. We try to protect ourselves against this negative power by inventing stratagems, ruses of language and of thought that hide an irrevocable fall. The existence of these strategies reveals the supremacy of the negative power they are trying to circumvent. For all his apparent lucidity, Mallarmé was mystified by this philosophical blindness until he recognized the illusory character of the dialectic on which he had founded his poetic strategy. In his last work, consciousness as well as natural objects are threatened by a power that exists on a more fundamental level than either of them.

And yet, even beyond this destruction of the self, the work can remain in existence. In Mallarmé's final poem, survival is symbolized in the image of a constellation that seems to escape from the destruction to which everything else has succumbed. Interpreting the image of the constellation, Blanchot states that in the poem, "the dispersion takes on the form and appearance of unity." [11] The unity is first stated in spatial terms: Mallarmé literally depicts the typographical, spatial disposition of the words on the page. Creating a highly complex network of relationships between the words, he gives the illusion of a three-dimensional reading analogous to the experience of space itself. The poem

10. *Le Livre à venir* (Paris, 1959), p. 277.
11. *Ibid.* p. 286.

becomes "the material, sensory affirmation of the new space. It is this space become poem." [12] We have a late, extreme version of the attempt to make the semantic and the sensory properties of language coincide. As the words in the poem that designate a ship are grouped in the shape of a sinking sailboat, the meaning of language is represented in a material form. In *Un Coup de Dés*, however, such experimentations come very close to being a deliberate hoax. If we have actually moved beyond the antithesis between subject and object, then such pseudo-objective games can no longer be taken seriously. In a typically Mallarméan form of irony, the spatial resources of language are exploited to the full at the very moment that they are known to be completely ineffective. It is no longer valid to speak, with Blanchot, of the earth as a spatial abyss that, reversing itself, becomes the corresponding abyss of the sky in which "words, reduced to their own space, make this space shine with a purely stellar light." [13] The idea of a reversal, however, is essential, provided one understands the reversal no longer in a spatial sense but in a temporal sense, as an axis around which the metaphor of space revolves to disclose the reality of time.

Blanchot participates in the reversal as he gradually discovers the temporal structure of *Un Coup de Dés*. The central articulation of this poem is very clearly marked: near the middle of the text, Mallarmé shifts from Roman type to italics and inserts an extended episode beginning with the words "comme si." At that moment, we change from a temporality that follows the course of an event presented as if it were actually taking place, to another, prospective temporality that exists only as fiction, strictly in the mode of "comme si." The fictional time is included in the historical time, like the play within the play of the Elizabethan theater. This enveloping structure corresponds to the relationship between history and fiction. The fiction in no way changes the outcome, the destiny of the historical event. In the terms of Mallarmé's poem, it will not abolish the random power of chance; the course of events remains unchanged by this long grammatical *apposition* that continues over six pages. The outcome is determined from the start by the single word "jamais," pointing to a past that

12. *Ibid.* p. 287.
13. *Ibid.* p. 288.

precedes the beginning of the fiction and to a future that will
follow it. The purpose of the fiction is not to intervene directly:
it is a cognitive effort by means of which the mind tries to escape
from the total indetermination that threatens it. The fiction influences the mode of abolition of consciousness, not by opposing it,
but by mediating the experience of destruction; it interposes a
language that accurately describes it. "History," says Blanchot, "is
replaced by hypothesis." [14] Yet this hypothesis can derive its statement only from a knowledge that was already previously given,
and that asserts precisely the impossibility of overcoming the arbitrary nature of this knowledge. The verification of the hypothesis
confirms the impossibility of its elaboration. Fiction and the history
of actual events converge toward the same nothingness; the knowledge revealed by the hypothesis of fiction turns out to be a knowledge that already existed, in all the strength of its negativity, before
the hypothesis was construed. Knowledge of the impossibility of
knowing precedes the act of consciousness that tries to reach it.
This structure is a circular one. The prospective hypothesis, which
determines a future, coincides with a historical, concrete reality
that precedes it and that belong to the past. The future is changed
into a past, in the infinite regression that Blanchot calls a *ressassement*, and that Mallarmé describes as the endless and meaningless noise of the sea after the storm has destroyed all sign of life,
"l'inférieur clapotis quelconque."

But does this knowledge of the circular structure of fictional
language not have, in its turn, a temporal destiny? Philosophy is
well acquainted with the circularity of a consciousness that puts
its own mode of being into question. This knowledge complicates
the philosopher's task a great deal, but it does not spell the end
of philosophical understanding. The same is true of literature.
Many specifically literary hopes and illusions have to be given up:
Mallarmé's faith in the progressive development of self-consciousness, for example, must be abandoned, since every new step in
this progression turns out to be a regression toward a more and
more remote past. Yet it remains possible to speak of a certain
development, of a movement of becoming that persists in the

14. *Ibid.* pp. 291–92.

fictional world of literary invention. In a purely temporal world, there can be no perfect repetition, as when two points coincide in space. As soon as the reversal described by Blanchot has taken place, the fiction is revealed as a temporal movement, and the question of its direction and intent must again be asked. "Mallarmé's ideal Book is thus obliquely asserted in terms of the movement of change and development that expressed perhaps its real meaning. This meaning will be the very movement of the circle." [15] And elsewhere: "We necessarily always write the same thing over again, but the development of what remains the same has infinite richness in its very repetition." [16] Blanchot is very close here to a philosophical trend which tries to rethink the notion of growth and development no longer in organic but in hermeneutic terms by reflecting on the temporality of the act of understanding. [17]

Blanchot's criticism, starting out as an ontological meditation, leads back into the question of the temporal self. For him, as for Heidegger, Being is disclosed in the act of its self-hiding and, as conscious subjects, we are necessarily caught up in this movement of dissolution and forgetting. A critical act of interpretation enables us to see how poetic language always reproduces this negative movement, though it is often not aware of it. Criticism thus becomes a form of demystification on the ontological level that confirms the existence of a fundamental distance at the heart of all human experience. Unlike the recent Heidegger, however, Blanchot does not seem to believe that the movement of a poetic consciousness could ever lead us to assert our ontological insight in a positive way. The center always remains hidden and out of reach;

15. *Le Livre à venir,* p. 296.
16. *Ibid.* p. 276.
17. See, for example, Hans-Georg Gadamer, *Wahrheit und Methode* (Tübingen, 1960), second edition, pp. 250 ff. In *Sein und Zeit,* Heidegger is certainly one of those who have laid the groundwork for this form of thought in our century. The affinity between Blanchot and Heidegger, despite the divergence in their subsequent development, should be studied more systematically than has been done up till now. The French philosopher Levinas, in his opposition to Heidegger and in his influence on Blanchot, would have to play a prominent part in such a study. There exists a brief article by Levinas on Blanchot and Heidegger published in March 1956 in *Monde nouveau,* a now defunct review.

we are separated from it by the very substance of time, and we never cease to know that this is the case. The circularity is not, therefore, a perfect form with which we try to coincide, but a directive that maintains and measures the distance that separates us from the center of things. We can by no means take this circularity for granted: the circle is a path that we have to construct ourselves and on which we must try to remain. At most, the circularity proves the authenticity of our intent. The search toward circularity governs the development of consciousness and is also the guiding principle that shapes the poetic form.

This conclusion has brought us back to the question of the subject. In his interpretative quest, the writer frees himself from empirical concerns, but he remains a self that must reflect on its own situation. As the act of reading "had to leave things exactly as they were," he tries to see himself the way he really is. He can only do this by "reading" himself, by turning his conscious attention toward himself, and not toward a forever unreachable form of being. Blanchot finally reaches this same conclusion with reference to Mallarmé.

> How can [the Book] assert itself in conformity with the rhythm of its own constitution, if it does not get outside itself? To correspond with the intimate movement that determines its structure, it must find the outside that will allow it to make contact with this very distance. The Book needs a mediator. The act of reading performs the mediation. But not just any reader will do . . . Mallarmé himself will have to be the voice of this essential reading. He has been abolished and has vanished as the dramatic center of his work, but this very annihilation has put him into contact with the reappearing and disappearing essence of the Book, with the ceaseless oscillation which is the main statement of the work.[18]

The necessity for self-reading, for self-interpretation, reappears at the moment when Mallarmé rises to the level of insight that allows him to name the general structure of all literary consciousness. The suppression of the subjective moment in Blanchot, asserted in the form of the categorical impossiblity of self-reading, is only a

18. *Ibid.* p. 294.

preparatory step in his hermeneutic of the self. In this way, he frees his consciousness of the insidious presence of inauthentic concerns. In the askesis of depersonalization, he tries to conceive of the literary work, not as if it were a thing, but as an autonomous entity, a "consciousness without a subject." This is not an easy undertaking. Blanchot must eliminate from his work all elements derived from everyday experience, from involvements with others, all reifying tendencies that tend to equate the work with natural objects. Only when this extreme purification has been achieved, can he turn toward the truly temporal dimensions of the text. This reversal implies a return toward a subject that, in fact, never ceased to be present. It is significant that Blanchot reaches this conclusion only with reference to an author like Mallarmé, who came upon it obliquely and whose actual itinerary needs to be revealed by interpretation, the way a watermark becomes visible only when held to the light. When he is dealing with writers who have given a more explicit version of the same process, Blanchot refuses them his full understanding. He tends to rate explicit forms of insight with other inessential matters that serve to make everyday life bearable—such as society, or what he calls history. He prefers hidden truth to revealed insight. In his critical work, this theoretician of interpretation prefers to describe the act of interpretation rather than the interpreted insight. He wanted, in all likelihood, to keep the latter in reserve for his narrative prose.

VI

The Literary Self as Origin:
The Work of Georges Poulet

A few years hence, the discussions that give to the literary studies of today such a controversial and didactic tone, will have faded before the intrinsic value of works that, in spite of being works of criticism, are nevertheless literary achievements in the fullest sense of the term. The case of poets or novelists that would occasionally write criticism is far from unusual; in modern French literature alone one can think of a long line that goes from Baudelaire to Butor and that includes Mallarmé, Valéry, and Blanchot. The nature of this double activity has often been wrongly understood. One assumes that these writers, out of dilettant-ism or out of necessity, have from time to time deserted the more important part of their work to express their opinion on the writings of their predecessors or contemporaries—a little in the manner of retired champions evaluating the performance of younger athletes. But the reasons that prompted these writers to take up criticism have only a limited interest. What matters a great deal is that Baudelaire's *Essay on Laughter*, Mallarmé's *La Musique et les Lettres*, or Blanchot's *Le Chant des Sirènes* are more than equal in verbal and thematic complexity to a prose poem of the *Spleen de Paris*, a page of *Un Coup de Dés* or a chapter of *Thomas l'obscur*. We are not suggesting that the poetic or novelistic parts of these works exist on the same level as the critical prose, and that both are simply interchangeable without making essential distinctions. The line that separates them marks out two worlds that are by no means identical or even complementary. The precise itinerary of such a line, however, would in most cases reveal a more subterranean path than one might originally have suspected and would indicate that the critical and the poetic components are so closely intertwined that it is impossible to touch the one without coming into contact with the other. It can be said of these works that they carry a constitutive critical element within themselves, exactly as Friedrich Schlegel, at the onset of the nineteenth century, characterized all "modern" literature by the ineluctable presence of a critical dimension.[1] If this is true, then the opposite is just as likely, and critics can be granted the full authority of literary authorship. Some contemporary critics can already lay claim to such a distinction.

More than any other, the criticism of Georges Poulet conveys the impression of possessing the complexity and the scope of a genuine work of literature, the intricacy of a city which has its avenues, its dead-ends, its underground labyrinths and panoramic lookouts. For the last forty years, he has pursued a meditation that takes the whole of Western literature for its theme; the orientation of his thought has remained remarkably stable throughout, directed toward a totalization that constantly seemed about to be achieved. On the other hand, he has shown considerable mobility, constantly putting his thought into question, returning to its original premises and starting afresh, even in his most recent texts. The combination of dynamicism with stability may explain apparent contradictions between the public and the private side of Poulet's criticism. From its beginnings, in the early 1920's, until the five consecutive volumes of the *Studies on Human Time,* the progression of the work has been incessant, almost monumental. It seems

1. Athenäum Fragment, no. 238, p. 204 in Friedrich Schlegel, *Kritische Ausgabe,* Band II, *Charakteristiken und Kritiken* I (1796–1801), Hans Eichner, ed., 1967.

to be carried by a methodological self-assurance that readily accounts for its considerable influence and authority. This self-
assurance is by no means merely apparent; any study will have to
account for the positive strength of the method. But, especially in
the polemical mood that prevails for the moment, when every
critical attitude has to become at once a critical position, the outward rigidity may well mask the other side, the more intimate
aspect that keeps Poulet's work open-ended, problematic, irre-
ducibly personal, and incapable of being transmitted, affiliated as
it is with a historical tradition that bears only the most distant
relation to the quarrels of the hour. In the numerous conferences
and public debates on criticism that have taken place of late, the
position of Poulet has been a prominent one. It was possible to
achieve this, however, only by hardening and schematizing categories that are a great deal more flexible when applied to texts
than when used against other critical methods. For this reason,
we prefer not to begin our reading of Georges Poulet with the
systematic parts, but rather with the ambivalences, the depths and
uncertainties that make up his more hidden side. The relative
serenity of the method can be better understood in terms of the
difficult experience of truth that stands behind it. The reverse
road, starting out from the established assurances, runs the risk of
missing the essential point.

Georges Poulet himself invites us to search, in the study of a
writer, for his "point of departure," an experience that is both
initial and central and around which the entire work can be
organized. The "points of departure" differ in kind for each
author and define him in his individuality; the test of their rele-
vance consists in their ability to serve effectively as organizing
principle for all his writings, whatever their period or genre may
be (finished work, fragment, journal, letter, etc.). On the other
hand, it seems that only a body of writing that can be so grasped
and organized fully deserves to be called a "work." The point of
departure serves as a unifying principle within a single corpus
while also serving to differentiate between writers, or even between
periods of literary history.

It is tempting to consider Poulet's own itinerary in this manner, but it soon becomes clear that, in his case, the notion is not simple; the fact that it serves at the same time as a principle that unifies and as a principle that differentiates indicates a certain degree of complexity. This complexity, however, is not more problematic than the simultaneous unity and differentiation that one encounters in any action committed by a conscious subject. Greater difficulties arise from the need to define the point of departure as center as well as origin. As its name indicates, it can function as a temporal origin, as the point before which no previous moment exists that, with regard to the work, has to be taken into account. In temporal terms therefore, the point of departure is a moment entirely oriented toward the future and separated from the past. On the other hand, when it acts as a center, it no longer functions as a genetic but as a structural and organizing principle. Since the center organizes a substance that can have a temporal dimension (and this seems, at first sight, to be the case for literature as Poulet conceives it), it serves as a co-ordinating point of reference for events that do not coincide in time. This can only mean that the center permits a link between past and future, thereby implying the active and constitutive intervention of a past. In temporal terms, a center cannot at the same time also be an origin, a source. The problem does not exist in the same manner in space, where one can conceive of a center that could also, as in the case of the Cartesian axes of analytical geometry, be an origin. But then the origin is a purely formal concept devoid of generative power, a mere point of reference rather than a point of departure. "Source" and "center" are by no means *a priori* identical. A very productive tension can develop between them. The work of Georges Poulet grows under the impact of this tension and reaches, for this reason, into the hidden foundations of literature.

We encounter the problem of the center and the origin from Poulet's earliest writings on; it will never cease to haunt him, regardless of the later knowledge and mastery. He meets it first of all, not in an abstract and theoretical way, but as a young novelist confronted with the practical question of constructing a convincing narrative. In a very interesting article that dates back to 1924, the expression "point of departure" is frequently used, although often with a negative accent.[2] Poulet tries to define the *nouveau roman* of his era in opposition to his elders, Gide and Proust, and seems convinced that in narrative fiction there can be no true origin, since one is always dependent on previous events. The novelists engaged in "creating" a character by the description of acts and feelings that seem spontaneous must in fact already be in the possession of a preconceived scheme that more or less consciously serves as a principle of selection. The fluid, dynamic, and continuous world of the fictional narration must be preceded by a static and determined world that serves as its "point of departure"; between these two worlds, there can be no actual contact.

> The figure [of the acts that narrate a story] exists at all times. Before acting it is already formed. Its only movement is a gradual unfolding. It moves in order to breathe, to exist. Only after this preparatory labor can it begin to grow. One may be surprised in thus hearing a truth conceived simultaneously in two modes, that of *being* and that of *becoming,* without any effort on the part of the author to establish a link between them, to discover a factor that they could have in common. . . . We behold a hero who has been consciously selected, his acts precalculated and his behavior adapted to an adventure that was foreseen even before it came into being. We witness a point of departure, a birth, then a movement. The writer concentrates on a sudden, startling development to which he may come back later, or he gives us a slow and static preparation that proceeds by minute detail, an analysis, visible or hidden, involuntary at times, in which the idea of the action is contained, albeit in an amended, distorted way, integrated within an exposition but incommensurable with it.

Further, in the course of the same article, the so-called "classical" novel (the reference is to *Adolphe* and *Dominique*) is defined in

2. "A propos du Bergsonisme" in *Sélection,* April 1924, pp. 65–75. The essay purports to be a study on a volume edited by Albert Thibaudet entitled *Le Bergsonisme (Trente Ans de pensée française,* vol. III). The five quotations that follow are from this article.

terms of a similar discontinuity between the appearance of a unified action and a static, earlier *donnée:*

> A common action of which the successive phases are chosen in such a way as to suggest reciprocal coherence, demands the creation of a point of departure, a kind of postulate located in the character of the protagonist as well as in the setting of the future action. Prior to the novel itself, one has to invent another novel, entirely devoid of action, but that nevertheless contains the development of the plot in all its irrevocable logic; two different fictional constructions preside over the same subject. These constructions, however, are not only different but opposed, utterly irreconcilable within the usual movement of life. The first contains a point of departure, fully shaped characters, a stable past, a moral overtone; the other consists only of the actions that mark the development of characters, but it contains neither the characters themselves, nor their ultimate destiny.

These texts combine a clear knowledge of the requirements that govern the narrative techniques of fiction with a nostalgic desire to share in the generative strength of sources and origins. The need for composition, for articulation of discontinuous elements, is constantly asserted: "Every artist is in fact a *Homo faber* who can deliberately, by an act of his intelligence, achieve a 'willed, reasoned and systematic detachment' that, as well as a natural detachment, allows him to combine heterogeneous elements. We openly admit that composition and ornamentation depend on 'devices' and on 'tricks.' "[3] But, next to the need for composition, an entirely different need is finally asserted as being the writer's true project: rebelling against the artifice of a pseudo-continuous narrative, knowing that the story is in fact the result of a radical break between a present and an earlier world, he may choose instead to remain entirely passive. He gives himself up to the intuitive presence of the moment and, carried along by a deeper current that fuses past and present, object and subject, presence and distance, the writer hopes to reach a more funda-

3. A book review by Edmond Jaloux published around that time characterizes Georges Poulet as "concerned with the study of composition" (voué à l'étude de la composition), *Nouvelles littéraires,* November 26, 1927.

mental continuity, which is the continuity of the source, of the creative impulse itself.

> By an act of forgetting, like Proust forgetting the numberless ideas and memories that get in the way of his sensations, as well as by an act of trust in our sense-perceptions, akin to what Bergson calls sympathy, we can come to consider what takes place in ourselves as existing on the same plane as what takes place in the outside world. In the novel we dream of, the setting will actually be the only character. Then the images and we ourselves will come to life. We do not float, nor do we sink. We live at the very heart of the universe, and the universe is all that exists. We ourselves have vanished. . . . The relationships between things have grown highly delicate, like ever-moving shadows, the light ebb and flow of a barely perceptible flux. Everything changes. Nothing is beyond understanding because the very idea of understanding, the calculated need to *explain,* has vanished. It is almost like an act of faith of which we do not know whether it is rooted in ourselves or in nature. Everything changes, but we are not even aware of it because, caught in the change, we ourselves have become the change and all points of reference have gone. Time and space become one. A single impulse carries all things toward a final aim that lies beyond our knowledge. . . .

The intensity of the tone indicates that such passages express a genuine spiritual temptation that reaches well beyond momentary influence or intellectual fashions. At more than forty years' distance, the Bergsonian fervor of this terminology may seem slightly recondite, just as the attempts to put this aesthetic into practice in the novel that Poulet published around the same time now appear dated.[4] Yet one should remember the movement as a constant, one of the recurrent themes that reappear throughout the work.

It is perhaps a mistake to speak here of passivity. Pure passivity would imply the complete loss of all spatial and temporal direction in a universe both infinite and chaotic, comparable to the "neutralité identique du gouffre" that Mallarmé evokes in *Un Coup de Dés.* In Poulet's text, the disappearance of all "points of reference"

4. Georges Thialet (pseudonym for Georges Poulet), *La Poule aux oeufs d'or* (Emile Paul: Paris, 1927).

does not convey an entirely undifferentiated experience of reality. The fact that he uses terms such as "intention" or "élan," the persistence of a teleological vocabulary, indicates that the passivity is not a relaxation of consciousness but rather the reward a consciousness receives for being able to coincide with a truly originary movement. This makes it possible to speak, in such a case, of an authentic point of departure, instead of the false point of departure claimed by novelists who remain in fact dependent on the hidden presence of previous events.

The same fundamental temptation reappears, in various versions, in the criticism and the fiction of Georges Poulet until the publication, in 1949, of the first volume of *Études sur le temps humain*. Time already played a part in the 1924 article, although it appeared as a device by means of which the "classical" novelists concealed the artifice of an illusory continuity: "There are perhaps no novels that are more homogeneous, more continuous than [classical] novels. This is probably due to a third factor that artificially suspends the antinomy between space and duration. This is the *time* factor, perfectly artificial in itself, but the natural product of our intelligence. . . ." The conviction that temporality is a mask that the human intelligence can impose upon the face of reality will never reappear in the form of such a direct statement. But it remains another constant of Poulet's thought. He will forever preserve a degree of antinomy between time and duration, an antinomy that is in fact another version of the tension between the source (the origin of duration) and the center (the locus of temporal articulation).

In the still Bergsonian article of 1924, time appears as a degraded form of space and as an artifice of the mind. Not until the first volume of the *Études sur le temps humain* does it acquire a much deeper existential significance. The optimism of the earlier text, the act of faith which allows Poulet to speak of the creative impulse as if it were a spontaneous act of levitation ("we do not float, nor do we sink"), will be short-lived. The tone of the later text is much more somber; maybe the experience of the novelist in facing the internal difficulties of a genre of which he had so well understood the ambivalence played a part in this change of mood. Whatever the case may be, at the same moment that Poulet finds the format and the method that will allow for the full development of his critical powers, the confidence in a happy accord between the movements of the mind and those of the world is breaking down. It is replaced by an experience best expressed in a quotation from Nicole that appears in the introduction to the *Etudes sur le temps humain*: "We are like those birds that are air-borne but powerless to remain suspended without motion, hardly able to remain in the same place, because they lack something solid to support them and have insufficient strength and energy to overcome the weight that forces them downward." [5] Poulet seems to be sharing this very experience and to find it in most of the writers he studies, with increasing negativity as one progresses in the intellectual history of the West from the Middle Ages to the present. The awakening of consciousness always occurs as an awareness of the frailty of our link with the world. The *cogito,* in Poulet's thought, takes the form of a reawakened feeling of fundamental fragility, which is nothing else than the subjective experience of time. One should not forget, however, that this is not an original but a derived feeling, the correlative of an intent that aims at coinciding perfectly with the origin of things. The feeling of fragility and of contingency designates the mood of a consciousness in quest of its own movement of origination.

This explains why the kind of emotion that accompanies the *cogito,* the fact, for instance, that it occurs as a feeling of happiness or of distress, is of secondary importance. Some writers start out in a state of happiness. Rousseau's moment of initial sensation, for example, a moment of which the "state of nature" in his theoretical writings is a projection on a wider historical scale, is entirely positive: ". . . in the state of pure sensation which is at the same time pure activity and feeling of existence, man is perfectly happy. There are no tensions within him: he fills the universe and the universe fills him. . . . This tranquillity, a state of harmony with the self which is also a harmony with nature, constitutes the only true happiness, the only fulfillment that could be called absolute. . . ." [6] The same is true of a contemporary writer such as Julien Green:

5. *Etudes sur le temps humain* (Paris, 1950), vol. I, pp. xviii–xix.
6. *Ibid.* p. 163.

In the novels of Julien Green, despite the somber and anxiety-
ridden atmosphere, there always comes a moment in which
consciousness and happiness, self-awareness and sensation are
mysteriously joined in an experience which is the starting-
point, the apogee, or even the endpoint of their history. Suddenly, and almost always without apparent reason, his charac-
ters literally wake up to a state of bliss. And in discovering
happiness, they also discover themselves. They are suddenly
stirred by a "happiness without cause, that comes from nowhere and that traverses the soul as the wind traverses the
trees." [7]

In others, however, the same awakening of consciousness can be
intensely painful. Thus for Marcel Proust ". . . the first moment is not a moment of plenitude or of vigor. He does not feel
carried by his future possibilities or his present-day realities. His
feeling of emptiness is not due to something that fails in his
future, but to a gap in his past, something that *no longer* exists,
not something that does *not as yet* exist. It resembles the first moment of a being that has lost everything, that has lost himself as
if he were dead. . . ." [8] The same feeling of "le néant des choses
humaines" (Rousseau) in a somewhat different form, appears as
the point of departure of Benjamin Constant:

> What first appears in Benjamin Constant and threatens to be-
> come a permanent condition, is the absence of any desire to
> engage himself into life. . . . Man has no raison d'être. His
> existence has no meaning, and he is powerless to give it any.
> . . . Everything is settled from the start by the mere fact of
> his mortal condition. . . . The entire course of his life is
> determined by the event that marks its conclusion. Death and
> only death gives meaning to life—and this meaning is en-
> tirely negative.[9]

The initial mood, whether positive or negative, is the percepti-
ble symptom of a change that takes place in the mind when it
claims to have reached or rediscovered the place of its origin. In
the deceptive stability of everyday consciousness which, in reality,
is only a kind of stupor, the new departure acts like a sudden

7. *Mesure de l'instant* (Paris, 1968), p. 339.
8. *Etudes sur le temps humain,* vol. I, p. 364.
9. *Benjamin Constant (par lui-même)* (Editions du Seuil: Paris, 1968), p. 28.

reawakening, shocking us into the discontinuity of a genuine movement. Poulet finds himself in agreement with the French eighteenth-century usage of the word *mouvement* to designate any spontaneous emotion.[10] His "point of departure," experienced as a particularly strong emotional tension, is primarily a change, the discontinuous movement from one state of consciousness to another. It is not conceived as the setting-in-motion of a substance that had up till then been stationary, nor is it the movement of origination through which a nothingness turns into being; it appears much rather as the re-discovery of a permanent and pre-existent movement that constitutes the foundation of all things. Poulet often formulates this aspect of his thought most clearly with reference to eighteenth-century writers. Thus in the article on the abbé Prévost, in which the key-term of *instant de passage* (the moment as discontinuity) is defined in all its richness:

> The *instant de passage,* in Prévost, marks the sudden leap from one extreme to the other. It is the moment at which both extremes come together. It does not matter whether the leap occurs from the greatest joy to the deepest despair, or vice-versa. . . . In no way does the term describe a lasting state of mind; it is an *état de passage,* less a state than a movement, the motion by which, within the same moment, the mind passes from one situation to its precise opposite.[11]

The term is crucially important, not only as a theoretical concept among others that are perhaps more forcefully stated, but for Poulet's critical practice as well. Present from the beginning, it starts to take final shape from the first volume of the *Etudes sur le temps humain* on; in his introduction to this volume, Poulet had stated that "the major discovery of the eighteenth century was the phenomenon of memory," yet it is the concept of instantaneity that finally emerges, often against and beyond memory, as the main insight of the book. The *instant de passage* supplants memory or, to be more precise, supplants the naïve illusion that memory would be capable of conquering the distance that separates the present from the past moment. Poulet's moment is "precisely what

10. *Le Dictionnaire de l'Académie* of 1762 defines "mouvement" as follows: "Se dit . . . des différentes impulsions, passions ou affections de l'âme."
11. *Etudes* . . . , pp. 148–52.

keeps different times from joining while nevertheless making it possible that they exist in succession . . . [man] lives in a present rooted in nothing, in a time that nowise relates to an earlier time. . . ." [12] Memory becomes important as failure rather than as achievement and acquires a negative value that gradually emerges from the critical essays of that period. The illusion that continuity can be restored by an act of memory turns out to be merely another moment of transition. Only the poetic mind can gather scattered fragments of time into a single moment and endow it with generative power.

Henceforth, Poulet's criticism will be organized around this moment, or around a sequence of such moments. His methodological assurance stems from the possibility of constructing and justifying a pattern that can encompass the entire work within the relatively narrow space of a coherent critical narrative, starting out from an initial situation and moving through a series of peripeties and discoveries to a conclusion that is satisfactory because it is prefigured. This narrative line does not follow that of the author's life, nor does it follow the chronological order of his writings; some of Poulet's books preserve the chronological order of traditional literary history and use it to some advantage, yet this order could be abandoned without anything essential being lost.[13] The critical narration has no reference to anything outside

12. *Ibid.* pp. 148–51.
13. The diachronic order of certain texts, such as the general introductions to the first *Etudes sur le temps humain* and especially to *Les Métamorphoses du cercle,* may create the impression that Poulet tends toward writing a general history of consciousness. But this is not really the case. The unity of his thought exists on the ontological and on the methodological level, not with regard to history. Since he conceives of literature as an eternally repeated sequence of new beginnings, no meaningful relationship can exist between the particularized narrative that traces the itinerary of a writer *ab ovo* and the collective narrative that aims to describe the cumulative movement of history. Some historical articulations can be described as if they were collective *moments de passage,* altogether similar in structure to the points of departure of an individual *cogito.* But the historical framework is kept only as a principle of classification without intrinsic significance. A rare attempt is made, as in the study on Proust that concludes the first volume of the *Etudes sur le temps humain,* to integrate an individual development within the historical scheme announced in the preface. The example, however, remains an isolated one. The light that Poulet's method can throw on literary history is at most a byproduct of its activity, certainly not its main principle.

the work and is constructed from the entirety of the writer's texts surveyed as in a panoramic view. It is articulated, however, around a number of centers without which it could not have taken shape. The plot of this critical narrative falls into an almost uniform pattern, which does not prevent individual or group variations but defines, in its uniformity, a literary consciousness as distinct from other forms of consciousness.

For all their basic uniformity, the various critical narratives are organized in terms of a series of dramatic events: reversals, repetitions, about-faces, and resolutions, each corresponding to a particular *moment de passage*. The original *cogito* is one of these moments. It is followed by a series of similar events in situations of greater or lesser complexity compared with the original impulse. Readers of Poulet are familiar with rebounding actions that, by a sudden change in direction, can turn the most desperate-looking impasse into an avenue of hope, or vice versa. In the study on Benjamin Constant, Constant's nihilism is so convincingly described that it seems impossible to imagine a force strong enough to rouse him from his prostration. Yet, a few pages later, we learn of a moment "that recurs from time to time and that enables him to break entirely with his former life." Constant seems to possess a faculty for radical reversal that cannot be explained, since it represents the very essence of discontinuity, but that can alter the most desperate situation. "We can say that every man carries within him the capacity to reverse the course of destiny an indefinite number of times" [14]—after which Constant finds himself "suddenly active and passionately interested, not only by the matter that holds his attention at the moment, but by everything that is alive in his vicinity." The reversal, brought about by mere chance, is followed by the reawakening of a consciousness reflecting on the miraculous nature of this event. By the same token, in a new *moment de passage*, "his thought passes from negative to positive, from a *no* to a *yes*." [15] A period of great literary productivity ensues, until, in this particular case, a final reversal takes him back to the depressed indifference that existed at the beginning. The itinerary is made up of a sequence of moments, each

14. *Benjamin Constant*, p. 54.
15. *Ibid.* p. 67.

erasing entirely whatever came before. The critic, however, can only construct and cover this itinerary because he strings on the imaginary time-thread of his narrative discontinuous but successive states of mind, joined together by the *moments de passage* that lead from one state to the next.

The temporal structure of this process becomes particularly clear in the texts dealing with Marcel Proust. In a series of studies that stretch over several years, Poulet will come closer and closer to defining the movement of Proust's mind. The development of the essays (as well as Proust's own development) is presented as a sequence of reversals in the novelist's outlook on time. At first, caught in the barrenness of his consciousness, Proust turns toward the past in the hope of finding there a firm and natural link between himself and the world. Had this quest for the remembered past been successful, he would have discovered the power to make the past into the strongest possible support of his existence. In a first reversal, it soon appears that this is not the case. The power of memory does not reside in its capacity to resurrect a situation or a feeling that actually existed, but it is a constitutive act of the mind bound to its own present and oriented toward the future of its own elaboration. The past intervenes only as a purely formal element, as a reference or a leverage that can be used because it is different and distant rather than because it is familiar and near. If memory allows us to enter into contact with the past, it is not because the past acts as the source of the present, as a temporal continuity that had been forgotten and of which we are again made aware; the remembrance does not reach us carried by a temporal flux; quite to the contrary, it is a deliberate act establishing a relation between two distinct points in time between which no relationship of continuity exists. Remembrance is not a temporal act but an act that enables a consciousness "to find access to the intemporal" [16] and to transcend time altogether. Such transcendence leads to the rejection of all that precedes the moment of remembrance as misleading and sterile in its deceptive relationship to the present. The power of invention has entirely passed into the present subject as it shows itself capable of creating relationships

16. *Etudes* . . . , p. 394.

that are no longer dependent on past experience. The point of departure was originally a moment of anxiety and of weakness because it felt no longer supported by anything that came before; it has now freed itself from the deceptive weight under which it was laboring and has become the creative moment par excellence, the source of Proust's poetic imagination as well as the center of the critical narrative by means of which Poulet makes us share in the adventure of this creation. This critical narrative turns around the central affirmation: "time recovered is time transcended."

The transcendence of time can only become a positive force if it is capable of re-entering, in turn, into the temporal process. It has freed itself from a rejected past, but this negative moment is now to be followed by a concern with the future that engenders a new stability, entirely distinct from the continuous and Bergsonian duration of memory. In the volume entitled *Le Point de départ,* the priority of the creative moment over the past, transposed into literary history, becomes an explicit concern with the future existence of the work. Such a concern was entirely lacking in the 1949 essay in which Proust's novel is said to be "without duration" or "covering the duration of a retrospective existence." Whereas, in the 1968 essay, "the work of literature . . . reveals how it passes from an instantaneous temporality, i.e. a sequence of detached events that make up the narrative, to a structural temporality, i.e. the gradual cohesion that unites the different parts. . . ." "The time of the work of art is the very movement by which the work passes from a formless and instantaneous to a formed and lasting state." [17] We are, in fact, witnessing a new *moment de passage* that will again reverse the perspective. At the start, a deceptive priority of the past over present and future was being asserted; this stage was followed by the discovery that the actual poetic power resides in a time-transcending moment: "It is not time that is given us, but the moment. With the given moment, it is up to us to make time." But since the moment then becomes reintegrated within time, we return in fact to a temporal activity, no longer based on memory but on the future-engendering

17. *Le Point de départ* (Paris, 1964), p. 40.

power of the mind. Thus the 1968 study on Marcel Proust is the exact reversal of its 1949 predecessor. The outlook toward the past is replaced by an equally passionate outlook toward the future which will have to experience its own disappointments, find its own strategies, and reach its own tentative solutions. Yet it could not be said that these two texts are in any way contradictory. They do not set up scales of value or make normative statements about an assumed superiority of future over past. Their interest stems instead from the movement generated by their dialectical interplay. The assertion of a future-engendering time, capable of duration, is certainly an important statement in itself, but it counts less by what it asserts than by what it represents: another *moment de passage* allowing for a new episode in the unending narrative of literary invention.

By thus singling out the notion of *moment de passage* as the main structural principle of Poulet's criticism, it may seem that we have definitely substituted the center for the source. We may have reintroduced time in a manner that was already being denounced in Poulet's earliest articles as contrary to his deepest spiritual leanings. Although the writer's experience of his past is being rejected, the fact remains that no critical discourse could come into being without the intervention of this past—just as the 1924 novelist could not construct a narrative that would not be founded, whether he wanted it or not, on a pattern that, for being prefigurative, nonetheless originated prior to the actual work. Should we conclude that Poulet had to forsake his fundamental project out of methodological necessity, that he had to renounce his desire to coincide with originating movements of thought in order to construct a coherent critical narrative?

The question cannot be considered without taking into account the complex relation in Poulet's work between the author and the reader of a given text. Like all truly literary works, his takes as its theme the choice it had to make between various modes of literary expression; no wonder, therefore, that it reflects the latent tension between poet (or novelist) and critic, especially with regard to their respective experiences of human time.

A critic has the possibility of seeing himself as a mediator who gives presence to an originating force. Something that predates

him in time is given him *a priori:* there can be no criticism without the prior existence of a text. And the tension between origin
and anteriority develops only when the source as well as the events
that are prior to it are located within the same person, when origin
and anteriority stem from a mind that is itself in quest of its
origin. This was the case in the earlier texts in which Poulet is
both novelist and critic. One remembers how the young novelist
of 1924 rebelled most of all against the deliberate and self-willed
aspects of the hidden world that preceded the beginning of his
narrative. An almost perverse streak of the human mind seems to
prevent an origin from coming into being; whenever this is about
to occur, the mind feels compelled to invent an earlier past that
deprives the event of its status origin. The novel that seemed to
flow freely from its own source thus lost all spontaneity, all genuine
originality. Things are quite different when the earlier past, the
passé antérieur, is initiated by someone else. The source is then
transferred from our own mind into that of another, and nothing
prevents us from considering this other mind as a genuine origin.
This happens in literary criticism, especially when one stresses the
element of identification that is part of all critical reading.

In the more general essays on method that Poulet has recently
been writing[18] the notion of identification plays a very prominent
part. Reading becomes an act of self-immolation in which the
initiative passes entirely into the hands of the author. The critic,
in Poulet's words, becomes the "prey" of the author's thought and
allows himself to be entirely governed by it. This complete sur-
render to the movement of another mind is the starting point of
the critical process. "I begin by letting the thought that invades
me . . . reoriginate within my own mind, as if it were reborn
out of my own annihilation." [19] This is said with reference to
Charles du Bos, but there can be little doubt that, in this essay
on one of his predecessors, Poulet speaks more than anywhere
else in his own name. In criticism, the *moment de passage* changes

18. Written as studies of individual critics (Rivière, Du Bos, Bachelard,
Blanchot, Marcel Raymond, Starobinski, etc.), these essays will eventually be
gathered into a volume on contemporary criticism.
19. "La pensée critique de Charles du Bos," *Critique,* 217, June 1965, pp. 491–
516.

from a temporal into an intersubjective act or, to be more precise, into the total replacement of one subject by another. We are, in fact, dealing with a substitutive relationship, in which the place of a self is usurped by another self. Proclaiming himself a passage-way (*lieu de passage*) for another person's thought, the critic evades the temporal problem of an anterior past. Nothing pre-vents the work from acquiring the status of an absolute origin. Poulet can then legitimately apply to the critic what Du Bos said of the poet: "He is the one who receives or, better, who endures. He is a meeting point (*point d'intersection*) rather than a center." With the experience of identification so defined, the problem of the center has, in fact, been eliminated, since the center is now entirely replaced by the authority of the originary source, which determines all the aspects and dimensions of the work. Poulet nevertheless continues to speak of the critic's relationship with his source in a vocabulary that derives from interpersonal relation-ships. He avoids all reference to biographical or psychological ele-ments, yet a literary work remains for him quite unambiguously the production of a person. Hence the presence, in his theoretical articles, of a hierarchical language in which the relationship be-tween author and reader is stated in terms of superiority and in-feriority: "the relationship [between author and reader] necessarily implies a special distinction between the one who gives and the one who receives, a relationship of superiority and inferiority." [20] "By becoming a critic . . . I find access to a new subjectivity. We could say that I allow myself to be replaced by some one better than myself." [21] Hence also some allusions that confer upon criti-cism a redeeming power that makes it akin to an act of personal grace. For if it is true that the particular subject that presides over the invention of a work is present in this work as a unique and absolute source, and if we can, in our turn, coincide entirely with this source in the act of critical identification, then literature would indeed be "the place where the person must be metamorphosed into a temple." [22] The fulfillment that was expected, in 1924, from abandoning oneself passively to the *élan vital* that animates

20. *Ibid.* p. 501.
21. *Les Chemins actuels de la critique* (Plon: Paris, 1967), p. 478.
22. "La pensée . . . ," *op. cit.* p. 515.

the universe finds its exact equivalence, after forty years, in the abandon with which the critic relinquishes his own self in his encounter with the work. In each case, the same quest for the experience of origination is lived with all the intensity of a truly spiritual aspiration.

But these theoretical texts on fellow critics or on criticism in general fail to define Poulet's own critical practice. The originality of his approach stems from the fact that he does not content himself with merely receiving works as if they were gifts, but that he participates, much more than he claims to do, in the problematic possibility of their elaboration. If one can speak of identification in his case, it is in a very different way than one would for Du Bos or Jean-Pierre Richard who can, at times, become one with the material or spiritual substance of the work. Whereas Poulet identifies himself with the project of its constitution; this is to say, his point of view is not so much that of the critic—as he himself defines it—as that of the writer. Consequently, the entire problem of anteriority and origin is not met as in the substitutive scheme which calls upon another to intervene, but is experienced from the inside, as seen by a subject that has delegated none of its inventive power to anyone else. Poulet often succeeds, in the course of a single article, in renewing entirely the interpretation of a given author. He can do so because he reaches as by instinct into the nearly inaccessible zone where the possibility of a work's existence is being decided. His criticism allows us to take part in a process that, far from being the inexorable development of an impulse that none could resist, appears as extremely vulnerable, likely to go astray at any moment, always threatened with error and aberration, risking paralysis or self-destruction, and forever obliged to start again on the road that it had hoped to have covered. It succeeds best of all when it deals with writers who have felt this fragility most acutely. Poulet can reach the quality of genuine subjectivity because, in his criticism, he is willing to undermine the stability of the subject and because he refuses to borrow stability for the subject from outside sources.

Significantly enough, in the most revealing passage of the Du Bos study, the presumed identification with another turns out to be the outward symptom of a division that takes place within the

self: "It often happens . . . that the outburst of life that occurs
with such admirable consequences, no longer seems to be the
result of an outside influence, but the manifestation within the
actual, inferior self of some earlier and superior self identified with
our very soul." [23] But how are we to understand a movement
which allows for a superior or "deeper" self to take the place of
an actual self, in accordance with a scheme of which the encounter
between author and critic was only the symbolical prefiguration?
One can say, with Poulet, that between these two selves, "relationships are born, revelations carried over and a marvelous receptivity
from mind to mind made to prevail." [24] Nevertheless, this relationship exists first of all in the form of a radical questioning of the
actual, given self, extending to the point of annihilation. And the
medium within which and by means of which this questioning
can take place can only be language, although Poulet hardly ever
designates it explicitly by that name. What was here being described as a relationship between two subjects designates in fact
the relationship between a subject and the literary language it
produces.

A far-reaching change of the temporal structure results from
this. The *instant de passage,* the decisive importance of which
has been so strongly in evidence, now turns out to create a dis-
junction within the subject. On the temporal level, this disjunc-
tion takes the form of a sudden reversal from a retrospective to a
future-oriented attitude of mind. However, the dimension of futurity that is thus being engendered exists neither as an empirical
reality nor in the consciousness of the subject. It exists only in
the form of a written language that relates, in its turn, to other
written languages in the history of literature and criticism. In this
way we can see Marcel Proust clearly separate a past or a present
that precedes the act of writing from a future that exists only in a
purely literary form. Proust mentions certain sensations or emotions that will only become important in retrospect when these
same events will recur as part of an interpretative process. "If, in
the *Recherche,* the hero's experience is already over at the time
that the novel begins, the knowledge of this experience, its mean-

23. *Ibid.* p. 502.
24. *Ibid.* p. 503.

ing and the use that can be made of it remain in suspense until the end, that is to say until a certain event has taken place that makes the future into more than just the point of arrival of the past, but into the point from where the past, seen in retrospect, gains meaning and intention." [25] In Proust's case, we know exactly what this decisive event was: the decision to write *A la recherche du temps perdu,* to pass from experience to writing, with all the risks this involves for the person of the writer. The explicit decision of Marcel Proust recurs in each writer; each one has invested his future existence once and forever into the project of his work.[26]

Why then does Poulet treat language, as a constitutive category of the literary consciousness, with a discretion that amounts to distrust? It takes a certain amount of interpretative labor to show that his criticism is actually a criticism of language rather than a criticism of the self.[27] His reserve can partly be explained by tactical considerations and by the desire to avoid misunderstandings. Poulet seems very eager to separate himself from other methods that give a prominent place to literary language, albeit for very different reasons. He is as remote from an impressionistic aestheticism that uses language as an object of sensation and pleasure, as from a formalism that would give it an autonomous and

---

25. *Mesure . . . ,* pp. 334–35.
26. Things seemed to be different in an earlier, more clearly theocentric period, when literary language could put itself directly in the service of religious experience. In the historical scheme presented by Poulet, this is no longer the case, ever since the increased secularization that took place in the eighteenth century. This historical view, certainly far from original in itself, is perhaps only brought in to justify Poulet's fundamental commitment to the literary vocation, a commitment that never wavers. If, during the seventeenth century, no incompatibility exists between the quest for the true Self that takes place in literature and in religious thought, this raises the dignity and the effectiveness of the literary act to a level that no subsequent event will be able to lower. Poulet's thought does not spring from a nostalgia for the theological vigor of the seventeenth century that he knows and understands so well; much rather, it asserts the fact that the main part of this energy is preserved later on in the manifestations of literary genius. Racine could still be theologian as well as poet; the same could no longer be true of Rousseau, less still of Proust. Yet, what Racine, Rousseau, and Proust have in common and what gives their work the power to last, belongs properly to their vocation as writers and is therefore irrevocably bound up with their literary project.
27. This is also the opinion of Gérard Genette, who rates Georges Poulet among the critics of interpretation (*Figures,* Paris 1966, p. 158).

objective status. And, in the present historical picture, these may well be the first tendencies that come to mind when one speaks of critical methods that put the main emphasis on language.

Yet his distrust of language has other causes that take us back to his more fundamental problems. Language clearly matters to him only when it gives access to a deeper subjectivity, as opposed to the scattered mood of common, everyday existence. The question remains whether this deeper self must be considered as an origin or as a center, as a source or as a reorientation of the mind from the past toward the future. In the first case, the self could coincide with a movement of origination and language could disappear into pure transparency. Literature would then tend to consume itself and become superfluous in the assertion of its own success. The only thing that jeopardizes it would be its dispersion within the facticity of the world, but this does not threaten its real core.

A conception of literature as a language of authenticity, similar to what is found, for example, in some of Heidegger's texts after *Sein und Zeit* is not Poulet's. He remains far removed from any form of prophetic poeticism. The quest for the source, which we have found constantly operative in his thought, can never be separated from the concern for the self that is the carrier of this quest. Yet this self does not possess the power to engender its own duration. This power belongs to what Poulet calls "the moment," but "the moment" designates, in fact, the point in time at which the self accepts language as its sole mode of existence. Language, however, is not a source; it is the articulation of the self and language that acquires a degree of prospective power. Self and language are the two focal points around which the trajectory of the work originates, but neither can by itself find access to the status of source. Each is the anteriority of the other. If one confers upon language the power to originate, one runs the risk of hiding the self. This Poulet fears most of all, as when he asserts: "I want at all costs to save the subjectivity of literature." [28] But if the subject is, in its turn, given the status of origin, one makes it coincide with Being in a self-consuming identity in which lan-

28. *Chemins actuels* . . . , p. 251.

guage is destroyed. Poulet rejects this alternative just as categorically as he rejects the other, although much less explicitly. The concern for language can be felt in the tone of anguish that inhabits the whole of his work and expresses a constant solicitude for literary survival. The subject that speaks in the criticism of Georges Poulet is a vulnerable and fragile subject whose voice can never become established as a presence. This is the very voice of literature, here incarnated in one of the major works of our time.

VII

The Rhetoric of Blindness:
Jacques Derrida's Reading of Rousseau

". . . einen Text als Text ablesen zu können, ohne eine Interpretation dazwischen zu mengen, ist die späteste Form der
'inneren Erfahrung,'—vielleicht eine kaum mögliche. . . ."

(". . . to be able to read a *text as text* without the interference of an interpretation is the latest-developed form of
"inner experience,"—perhaps one that is hardly possible. . . ."
(Nietzsche, *Der Wille zur Macht,* 479)

Looking back over this first group of essays as a representative though deliberately one-sided selection from contemporary
literary criticism, a recurrent pattern emerges. A considerable
amount of insight into the distinctive nature of literary language
can be gained from writers such as Lukács, Blanchot, Poulet, or
the American New Critics, but not by way of direct statement, as
the explicit assertion of a knowledge derived from the observation
or understanding of literary works. It is necessary, in each case,
to read beyond some of the more categorical assertions and balance
them against other much more tentative utterances that seem to
come close, at times, to being contradictory to these assertions. The
contradictions, however, never cancel each other out, nor do they
enter into the synthesizing dynamics of a dialectic. No contradiction or dialectical movement could develop because a fundamental

difference in the level of explicitness prevented both statements from meeting on a common level of discourse; the one always lay hidden within the other as the sun lies hidden within a shadow, or truth within error. The insight seems instead to have been gained from a negative movement that animates the critic's thought, an unstated principle that leads his language away from its asserted stand, perverting and dissolving his stated commitment to the point where it becomes emptied of substance, as if the very possibility of assertion had been put into question. Yet it is this negative, apparently destructive labor that led to what could legitimately be called insight.

Even among the few examples of this short list, significant variations occur in the degree of complexity of the process. In a case such as Lukács's *Essay on the Novel*, we came close to open contradiction. Two explicit and irreconcilable statements face each other in a pseudo-dialectic. The novel is first defined as an ironic mode condemned to remain discontinuous and contingent; the type of totality claimed for the form therefore has to differ in essence, and even in appearance, from the organic unity of natural entities. Yet the tone of the essay itself is not ironical but elegiac: it never seems able to escape from a concept of history that is itself organic, tributary of an original source—the Hellenic epic—that knew neither discontinuity nor distance and, potentially, contained the entirety of the later development within itself. This nostalgia ultimately leads to a synthesis in the modern novel— Flaubert's *Education sentimentale*—in which the unity is recaptured beyond all the negative moments it contains. The second assertion, that "Time confers upon it [the *Education sentimentale*] the appearance of organic growth," stands in direct contradiction to the first, which allows for no such apparent or actual resemblance with organic forms.

It is not a matter of indifference that the mediating category through which this synthesis is presumably achieved is precisely time. Time acts as the healing and reconciling force against an estrangement, a distance that seems to be caused by the arbitrary intervention of a transcendental force. A slightly tighter exegetic pressure on the text reveals that this transcendental agent is itself temporal and that what is being offered as a remedy is in fact the

disease itself. A negative statement about the essentially problematical and self-destructive nature of the novel is disguised as a
positive theory about its ability to rejoin, at the end of its dialectical
development, a state of origin that is purely fictional, though fal-
laciously presented as having historical existence. A certain concept, time, is made to function on two irreconcilable levels: on the
organic level, where we have origin, continuity, growth, and
totalization, the statement is explicit and assertive; on the level
of ironic awareness, where all is discontinuous, alienated, and
fragmentary, it remains so implicit, so deeply hidden behind error
and deception, that it is unable to rise to thematic assertion. The
crucial link between irony and time is never made in Lukács's
essay. And yet, it is the existence of this link that the text finally
conveys to the mind of the reader. The three crucial factors in
the problem have been identified and brought into relationship
with each other: organic nature, irony, and time. To reduce the
novel, as an instance of literary language, to the interplay among
these three factors is an insight of major magnitude. But the manner in which the three factors are said to relate to each other, the
plot of the play they are made to perform, is entirely wrong. In
Lukács's story, the villain—time—appears as the hero, when he
is in fact murdering the heroine—the novel—he is supposed to
rescue. The reader is given the elements to decipher the real plot
hidden behind the pseudo-plot, but the author himself remains
deluded.

In the other instances, the pattern, though perhaps less clear,
is closely similar. The American New Critics arrived at a description of literary language as a language of irony and ambiguity
despite the fact that they remained committed to a Coleridgian
notion of organic form. They disguised a foreknowledge of
hermeneutic circularity under a reified notion of a literary text
as an objective "thing." Here it is the concept of form that is made
to function in a radically ambivalent manner, both as a creator
and undoer of organic totalities, in a manner that resembles the
part played by time in Lukács's essay. The final insight, here
again, annihilated the premises that led up to it, but it is left to
the reader to draw a conclusion that the critics cannot face if they
are to pursue their task.

Similar complications arise when the question of the specificity of literary language is seen from a perspective that is neither historical, as in Lukács, nor formal, as in the American New Criticism, but centered in a self, in the subjectivity of the author or of the author-reader relationship. The category of the self turns out to be so double-faced that it compels the critic who uses it to retract implicitly what he affirms and to end up by offering the mystery of this paradoxical movement as his main insight. Acutely aware of the frailty and fragmentation of the self in its exposure to the world, Binswanger tries to establish the power of the work of art as a sublimation that can lead, despite persistent dangers, to a balanced structurization of multiple tensions and potentialities within the self. The work of art thus becomes an entity in which empirical experiences and their sublimation can exist side by side, through the mediating power of a self that possesses sufficient elasticity to encompass both. In the end he suggests the existence of a gap separating the artist as an empirical subject from a fictional "self." This fictional self seems to exist in the work, but can only be reached at the cost of reason. In this way the assertion of a self leads by inference to its disappearance.

Writing on a more advanced level of awareness, the disappearance of the self becomes the main theme of Blanchot's critical work. Whereas it seems impossible to assert the presence of a self without in fact recording its absence, the thematic assertion of this absence reintroduces a form of selfhood, albeit in the highly reductive and specialized form of a self-reading. And if the act of reading, potential or actual, is indeed a constitutive part of literary language, then it presupposes a confrontation between a text and another entity that seems to exist prior to the elaboration of a subsequent text and that, for all its impersonality and anonymity, still tends to be designated by metaphors derived from selfhood. Claiming to speak for this universal but strictly literary subject, Poulet asserts its power to originate its own temporal and spatial world. It turns out, however, that what is here claimed to be an origin always depends on the prior existence of an entity that lies beyond reach of the self, though not beyond the reach of a language that destroys the possibility of origin.

All these critics seem curiously doomed to say something quite

different from what they meant to say. Their critical stance—
Lukács's propheticism, Poulet's belief in the power of an original
cogito, Blanchot's claim of meta-Mallarméan impersonality—is
defeated by their own critical results. A penetrating but difficult
insight into the nature of literary language ensues. It seems,
however, that this insight could only be gained because the critics
were in the grip of this peculiar blindness: their language could
grope toward a certain degree of insight only because their method
remained oblivious to the perception of this insight. The insight
exists only for a reader in the privileged position of being able
to observe the blindness as a phenomenon in its own right—the
question of his own blindness being one which he is by definition
incompetent to ask—and so being able to distinguish between
statement and meaning. He has to undo the explicit results of a
vision that is able to move toward the light only because, being
already blind, it does not have to fear the power of this light.
But the vision is unable to report correctly what it has perceived in
the course of its journey. To write critically about critics thus
becomes a way to reflect on the paradoxical effectiveness of a
blinded vision that has to be rectified by means of insights that it
unwittingly provides.

Several questions at once arise. Is the blindness of these critics
inextricably tied up with the act of writing itself and, if this is
so, what characteristic aspect of literary language causes blindness
in those who come into close contact with it? Or could the considerable complication of the process be avoided by writing about
literary texts instead of about critics, or about other, less subjective
critics? Are we perhaps dealing with pseudo-complexities, resulting
from an aberration restricted to a small group of contemporary
critics?

The present essay strives for a tentative answer to the first of
these questions. As for the others, they touch upon a recurrent
debate that underlies the entire history of literary criticism: the
latent opposition between what is now often called instrinsic versus
extrinsic criticism. The critics here assembled all have in common
a certain degree of immanence in their approach. For all of them,
the encounter with the language of literature involves a mental
activity which, however problematical, is at least to a point gov-

erned by this language only. All strive for a considerable degree of generality, going so far that they can be said to be writing, not about particular works or authors, but about literature as such. Nevertheless, their generality remains grounded in the initial act of reading. Prior to any generalization about literature, literary texts have to be read, and the possibility of reading can never be taken for granted. It is an act of understanding that can never be observed, nor in any way prescribed or verified. A literary text is not a phenomenal event that can be granted any form of positive existence, whether as a fact of nature or as an act of the mind. It leads to no transcendental perception, intuition, or knowledge but merely solicits an understanding that has to remain immanent because it poses the problem of its intelligibility in its own terms. This area of immanence is necessarily part of all critical discourse. Criticism is a metaphor for the act of reading, and this act is itself inexhaustible.

Attempts to circumvent or to resolve the problem of immanence and to inaugurate a more scientific study of literature have played an important part in the development of contemporary criticism. Perhaps the most interesting cases are authors such as Roman Jakobson, Roland Barthes, and even Northrop Frye, who are on the borderline between the two camps. The same is true of certain structuralist tendencies, which try to apply extrinsic methods to material that remains defined intrinsically and selectively as literary language. Since it is assumedly scientific, the language of a structuralist poetics would itself be definitely "outside" literature, extrinsic to its object, but it would prescribe (in deliberate opposition to describe) a generalized and ideal model of a discourse that defines itself without having to refer to anything beyond its own boundaries; the method postulates an immanent literariness of literature that it undertakes to prescribe.[1] The question remains whether the logical difficulties inherent in the act of interpretation can be avoided by thus moving from an actual, particular text to an ideal one. The problem has not always been correctly perceived, partly because the model for the act of interpretation is being constantly oversimplified.

1. T. Todorov, *Qu'est-ce que le structuralisme?* (Editions du Seuil: Paris, 1968), p. 102.

A recent example can serve as illustration. In a cogently argued and convincing plea for a structural poetics, Tszvestan Todorov dismisses intrinsic criticism in the following manner:

> . . . if one introduces the concept of immanence, a limitation quickly appears and puts into question the very principle of the description. To describe a work, whether literary or not, for itself and in itself, without leaving it for a moment, without projecting it on anything but itself—this is properly speaking impossible. Or rather: the task is possible, but it would make the description into a mere word-for-word repetition of the work itself. . . . And, in a sense, every work is itself its best description.[2]

The use of the term "description," even when taken with full phenomenological rigor, is misleading here. No interpretation pretends to be the description of a work, as one can speak of the description of an object or even of a consciousness, the work being at most an enigmatic appeal to understanding. Interpretation could perhaps be called the description of an understanding, but the term "description," because of its intuitive and sensory overtones, would then have to be used with extreme caution; the term "narration" would be highly preferable. Because the work cannot be said to understand or to explain itself without the intervention of another language, interpretation is never mere duplication. It can legitimately be called a "repetition," but this term is itself so rich and complex that it raises at once a host of theoretical problems. Repetition is a temporal process that assumes difference as well as resemblance. It functions as a regulative principle of rigor but asserts the impossibility of rigorous identity, etc. Precisely to the extent that all interpretation has to be repetition it also has to be immanent.

Todorov rightly perceives the very close connection between interpretation and reading. As he is, however, the captive of the notion of interpretation as duplication, Todorov blames the interpretative process for producing the divergence, the margin of error that is in fact its *raison d'être*:

> What comes closest of all to this ideal but invisible description is simply reading itself. . . . Yet the mere process of reading

is not without consequence: no two readings of the same book
are ever identical. In reading, we trace a passive type of writing, we add and suppress what we wish to find or to avoid
in the text. . . . What to say then of the no longer passive
but active form of reading that we call criticism? . . . How
could one write a text that remains faithful to another text and
still leaves it untouched; how could one articulate a discourse
that remains immanent to another discourse? From the moment there is writing and no longer mere reading, the critic
is saying something that the work he studies does not say,
even if he claims to be saying the same thing.[3]

Our readings have revealed even more than this: not only does
the critic say something that the work does not say, but he even
says something that he himself does not mean to say. The seman-
tics of interpretation have no epistemological consistency and can
therefore not be scientific. But this is very different from claiming that what the critic says has no immanent connection with
the work, that it is an arbitrary addition or subtraction, or that
the gap between his statement and his meaning can be dismissed
as mere error. The work can be used repeatedly to show where
and how the critic diverged from it, but in the process of showing this our understanding of the work is modified and the faulty
vision shown to be productive. Critics' moments of greatest blindness with regard to their own critical assumptions are also the
the moments at which they achieve their greatest insight. Todorov
correctly states that naïve and critical reading are in fact actual
or potential forms of "écriture" and, from the moment there is
writing, the newly engendered text does not leave the original
text untouched. Both texts can even enter into conflict with each
other. And one could say that the further the critical text pene-
trates in its understanding, the more violent the conflict becomes,
to the point of mutual destruction: Todorov significantly has to
have recourse to an imagery of death and violence in order to
describe the encounter between text and commentary.[4] One could

3. *Ibid.* p. 100.
4. *Ibid.* p. 101. ". . . pour laisser la vie à l'oeuvre, le texte descriptif doit
mourir; s'il vit lui-même, c'est qu'il tue l'oeuvre qu'il dit."

even go further still and see the murder become suicide as the critic, in his blindness, turns the weapon of his language upon himself, in the mistaken belief that it is aimed at another. In saying all this, however, no argument has been presented against the validity of intrinsic criticism; on the contrary, not only is the discrepancy between the original and the critical text granted, but it is given immanent exegetic power as the main source of understanding. Since they are not scientific, critical texts have to be read with the same awareness of ambivalence that is brought to the study of non-critical literary texts, and since the rhetoric of their discourse depends on categorical statements, the discrepancy between meaning and assertion is a constitutive part of their logic. There is no room for Todorov's notions of accuracy and identity in the shifting world of interpretation. The necessary immanence of the reading in relation to the text is a burden from which there can be no escape. It is bound to stand out as the irreducible philosophical problem raised by all forms of literary criticism, however pragmatic they may seem or want to be. We encounter it here in the form of a constitutive discrepancy, in critical discourse, between the blindness of the statement and the insight of the meaning.

The problem occupies, of course, a prominent place in all philosophies of language, but it has rarely been considered within the humbler, more artisan-like context of practical interpretation. "Close reading" can be highly discriminating and develop a refined ear for the nuances of self-conscious speech, but it remains curiously timid when challenged to reflect upon its own self-consciousness. On the other hand, critics like Blanchot and Poulet who make use of the categories of philosophical reflection tend to erase the moment of actual interpretative reading, as if the outcome of this reading could be taken for granted in any literate audience. In France it took the rigor and intellectual integrity of a philosopher whose main concern is not with literary texts to restore the complexities of reading to the dignity of a philosophical question.

Jacques Derrida makes the movements of his own reading an integral part of a major statement about the nature of language in general. His knowledge stems from the actual encounter with texts, with a full awareness of the complexities involved in such an encounter. The discrepancy implicitly present in the other critics here becomes the explicit center of the reflection. This means that Derrida's work is one of the places where the future possibility of literary criticism is being decided, although he is not a literary critic in the professional sense of the term and deals with hybrid texts—Rousseau's *Essai sur l'origine des langues,* Plato's *Phaedrus*—that share with literary criticism the burden of being partly expository and partly fictional. His commentary on Rousseau[5] can be used as an exemplary case of the interaction between critical blindness and critical insight, no longer in the guise of a semiconscious duplicity but as a necessity dictated and controlled by the very nature of all critical language.

Rousseau is one of the group of writers who are always being systematically misread. I spoke above of the blindness of critics with regard to their own insights, of the discrepancy, hidden to them, between their stated method and their perceptions. In the history as well as in the historiography of literature, this blindness can take on the form of a recurrently aberrant pattern of interpretation with regard to a particular writer. The pattern extends from highly specialized commentators to the vague *idées reçues* by means of which this writer is identified and classified in general histories of literature. It can even include other writers who have been influenced by him. The more ambivalent the original utterance, the more uniform and universal the pattern of consistent error in the followers and commentators. Despite the apparent alacrity with which one is willing to assent in principle to the notion that all literary and some philosophical language is essentially ambivalent, the implied function of most critical commentaries and some literary influences is still to do away at all costs with these ambivalences; by reducing them to contradictions, blotting out the disturbing parts of the work or, more subtly, by manipulating the systems of valorization that are operating within the texts. When, especially as in the case of Rousseau, the ambivalence is itself a part of the philosophical statement, this is

5. Jacques Derrida, *De la Grammatologie* (Éditions de Minuit: Paris, 1967), Part II, pp. 145–445. Henceforth referred to as *Gr.*

very likely to happen. The history of Rousseau interpretation is particularly rich in this respect, both in the diversity of the tactics employed to make him say something different from what he said, and in the convergence of these misreadings toward a definite configuration of meanings. It is as if the conspiracy that Rousseau's paranoia imagined during his lifetime came into being after his death, uniting friend and foe alike in a concerted effort to misrepresent his thought.

Any attempt to explain why and how this distortion took place would lead afield to considerations that do not belong in this context. We can confine ourselves to a single, trivial observation: in Rousseau's case, the misreading is almost always accompanied by an overtone of intellectual and moral superiority, as if the commentators, in the most favorable of cases, had to apologize or to offer a cure for something that went astray in their author. Some inherent weakness made Rousseau fall back into confusion, bad faith, or withdrawal. At the same time, one can witness a regaining of self-assurance in the one who utters the judgment, as if the knowledge of Rousseau's weakness somehow reflected favorably on his own strength. He knows exactly what ails Rousseau and can therefore observe, judge, and assist him from a position of unchallenged authority, like an ethnocentric anthropologist observing a native or a doctor advising a patient. The critical attitude is diagnostic and looks on Rousseau as if he were the one asking for assistance rather than offering his counsel. The critic knows something about Rousseau that Rousseau did not wish to know. One hears this tone of voice even in so sympathetic and penetrating a critic as Jean Starobinski, who did more than anyone else to free Rousseau studies from accumulated decades of wrong *idées reçues*. "No matter how strong the duties of his sympathy may be, the critic must understand [what the writer can not know about himself] and not share in this ignorance," [6] he writes, and although this claim is legitimate, especially since it applies, in this passage, to Rousseau's experiences of childhood, it is perhaps stated with a little too much professional confidence. The same critic goes on to suggest that the more paradoxical statements of Rousseau should not really be taken at face value:

6. Jean Starobinski, "Jean-Jacques Rousseau et le péril de la réflexion" in *L'Oeil vivant* (Gallimard: Paris, 1961), p. 98.

. . . it often happens that he overstates his aim and forces the meaning, in splendid sentences that can hardly stand the test of being confronted with each other. Hence the frequently repeated accusations of sophistry. . . . Should we take those lapidary maxims, those large statements of principle at face value? Should we not rather be looking beyond Jean-Jacques's words toward certain demands made by his soul, toward the vibration of his feelings? We do him perhaps a disservice when we expect him to provide rigorous coherence and systematic thought; his true presence is to be found, not in his discourse, but in the live and still undefined movements that precede his speech. . . .[7]

Benevolent as it sounds, such a statement reduces Rousseau from the status of philosopher to that of an interesting psychological case; we are invited to discard his language as "des phrases splendides" that function as a substitute for pre-verbal emotional states into which Rousseau had no insight. The critic can describe the mechanism of the emotions in great detail, drawing his evidence from these very "phrases splendides" that cover up a by no means splendid personal predicament.

At first sight, Derrida's attitude toward Rousseau seems hardly different. He follows Starobinski in presenting Rousseau's decision to write as an attempt at the fictional recovery of a plenitude, a unity of being that he could never achieve in his life.[8] The writer "renounces" life, but this renunciation is hardly in good faith: it is a ruse by means of which the actual sacrifice, which would imply the literal death of the subject, is replaced by a "symbolic" death that leaves intact the possibility of enjoying life, adding to it the possibility of enjoying the ethical value of an act of renunciation that reflects favorably on the person who performs it. The claim of the literary language to truth and generality is thus suspect from the start, based on a duplicity within a self that willfully creates a confusion between literal and symbolic action in order to achieve self-transcendence as well as self-preservation. The blindness of the subject to its own duplicity has psychological roots since the unwillingness to see the mechanism of self-deception is protective. A whole mythology of original innocence in a pre-

7. *Ibid.* p. 184.
8. *Gr.*, pp. 204–5.

reflective state followed by the recovery of this innocence on a more impersonal, generalized level—the story so well described by Starobinski in the Rousseau essay of *L'Oeil vivant*—turns out to be the consequence of a psychological ruse. It collapses into nothingness, in mere "phrases splendides," when the stratagem is exposed, leaving the critic to join ranks with the numerous other "juges de Jean-Jacques."

Even on this level, Derrida's reading of Rousseau diverges fundamentally from the traditional interpretation. Rousseau's bad faith toward literary language, the manner in which he depends on it while condemning writing as if it were a sinful addiction, is for Derrida the personal version of a much larger problem that cannot be reduced to psychological causes. In his relationship to writing, Rousseau is not governed by his own needs and desires, but by a tradition that defines Western thought in its entirety: the conception of all negativity (non-being) as absence and hence the possibility of an appropriation or a reappropriation of being (in the form of truth, of authenticity, of nature, etc.) as presence. This ontological assumption both conditions and depends on a certain conception of language that favors oral language or voice over written language (*écriture*) in terms of presence and distance: the unmediated presence of the self to its own voice as opposed to the reflective distance that separates this self from the written word. Rousseau is seen as one link in a chain that closes off the historical era of Western metaphysics. As such, his attitude toward language is not a psychological idiosyncrasy but a typical and exemplary fundamental philosophical premise. Derrida takes Rousseau seriously as a thinker and dismisses none of his statements. If Rousseau nevertheless stands, or seems to stand, indicted, it is because the entirety of Western philosophy is defined as the possibility of self-indictment in terms of an ontology of presence. This would suffice to exclude any notion of superiority on Derrida's part, at least in the interpersonal sense of the term.

Rousseau's assertion of the primacy of voice over the written word, his adherence to the myth of original innocence, his valorization of unmediated presence over reflection—all these are characteristics that Derrida could legitimately have derived from a long tradition of Rousseau interpreters. He wishes, however, to set himself apait fium those who reduce these myths to self-centered strategies of Rousseau's psyche and prefers to approach him by way of a disciple who is more orthodox than Rousseau himself in accepting at face-value dreams of the innocence and integrity of oral language. Derrida's main theme, the recurrent repression, in Western thought, of all written forms of language, their degradation to a mere adjunct or supplement to the live presence of the spoken word, finds a classical example in the works of Lévi-Strauss. The pattern in the passages from Lévi-Strauss that Derrida singles out for comment is consistent in all its details, including the valorization of music over literature and the definition of literature as a means to recoup a presence of which it is a distant and nostalgic echo, unaware that literature is itself a cause and a symptom of the separation it bewails.

Naïve in Lévi Strauss, the same assumptions become a great deal more devious and ambivalent when they appear in Rousseau himself. Whenever Rousseau designates the moment of unity that exists at the beginning of things, when desire coincides with enjoyment, the self and the other are united in the maternal warmth of their common origin, and consciousness speaks with the voice of truth, Derrida's interpretation shows, without leaving the text, that what is thus designated as a moment of presence always has to posit another, prior moment and so implicitly loses its privileged status as a point of origin. Rousseau defines voice as the origin of written language, but his description of oral speech or of music can be shown to possess, from the start, all the elements of distance and negation that prevent written language from ever achieving a condition of unmediated presence. All attempts to trace writing back to a more original form of vocal utterance lead to the repetition of the disruptive process that alienated the written word from experience in the first place. Unlike Lévi-Strauss, Rousseau "*in fact,* experienced the disappearance [of full presence] in the word itself, in the illusion of immediacy," [9] and he "recognized and analyzed [this disappearance] with incomparable astuteness." But Rousseau never openly declares this; he never asserts the disappearance of presence outright or faces its consequences. On the

9. *Gr.,* p. 203.

contrary, the system of valorization that organizes his writings favors the opposite trend, praises nature, origin, and the spontaneity of mere outcry, over their opposites, not only in the nostalgic, elegiac manner of a poetic statement that makes no claim to truth, but as a philosophical system. In the *Discours sur l'origine de l'inégalité,* in the *Essai sur l'origine des langues* and also later in *Emile* and the *Confessions,* Rousseau expounds the philosophy of unmediated presence that Lévi-Strauss took over uncritically and that Starobinski tries to demystify in the name of a later, perhaps less enlightened, version of the same philosophy. Derrida's considerable contribution to Rousseau studies consists in showing that Rousseau's own texts provide the strongest evidence against his alleged doctrine, going well beyond the point reached by the most alert of his modern readers. Rousseau's work would then reveal a pattern of duplicity similar to what was found in the literary critics: he "knew," in a sense, that his doctrine disguised his insight into something closely resembling its opposite, but he chose to remain blind to this knowledge. The blindness can then be diagnosed as a direct consequence of an ontology of unmediated presence. It remains for the commentator to undo, with some violence, the historically established pattern or, as Derrida puts it, the "orbit" of significant misinterpretation—a pattern of which the first example is to be found in Rousseau's own writings—and thus, by a process of "deconstruction," to bring to light what had remained unperceived by the author and his followers.

Within the orbit of my own question, the attention has to be directed toward the status of this ambivalent "knowledge" that Derrida discovers in Rousseau. The text of *De la Grammatologie* necessarily fluctuates on this point. At times, it seems as if Rousseau were more or less deliberately hiding from himself what he did not want to know: "Having, in a way . . . identified this power which, by opening up the possibility of speech, disrupts the subject that it creates, prevents it from being present to its own signs, saturates its speech with writing, Rousseau is nevertheless more eager to conjure it out of existence than to assume the burden of its necessity." [10] "Conjurer" (as well as the weaker

10. *Gr.,* p. 204.

"effacer" that is used elsewhere in the same context) supposes some awareness and, consequently, a duplicity within the self, a degree of deliberate self-deception. The ethical overtone of deceit, implying some participation of the will, is apparent in several other descriptions that use a vocabulary of transgression: "The replacement of mere stressed sound by articulated speech is the origin of language. The modification of speech by writing took place as an extrinsic event at the very beginning of language. It is the origin of language. Rousseau describes this without openly saying so. In contraband." [11] But at other moments it appears instead as if Rousseau were in the grip of a fatality that lies well beyond the reach of his will: "Despite his avowed intent [to speak of origins] Rousseau's discourse is governed (se laisse contraindre) by a complication that always takes on the form of an excess, a "supplement" to the state of origin. This does not eliminate the declared intent but *inscribes* it within a system that it no longer controls (qu'elle ne domine plus)." [12] "Se laisser contraindre" unlike "conjurer" or "effacer" is a passive process, forced upon Rousseau by a power that lies beyond his control. As the word, "inscrite" (italicized by Derrida), and the next sentence[13] make clear, this power is precisely that of written language whose syntax undermines the declarative assertion. Yet the act of "conjurer" also occurred by means of written language, so the model is not simply that of a pre-lingual desire that would necessarily be corrupted or overtaken by the transcendental power of language: language is being smuggled into a presumably languageless state of innocence, but it is by means of the same written language that it is then made to vanish: the magic wand that should "conjure" the written word out of existence is itself made of language. This double valorization of language is willed and controlled as the crux of Derrida's argument: only by language can Rousseau conquer language, and this paradox is responsible for the ambivalence of his attitude toward writing.[14] The exact epistemological status of

11. *Gr.*, p. 443.
12. *Gr.*, p. 345.
13. *Gr.*, p. 345. "The desire for origin becomes a necessary and unavoidable function [of language], but it is governed by a syntax that is without origin."
14. *Gr.*, p. 207.

this ambivalence cannot be clarified: things do not happen as if Rousseau were at least semi-conscious when engaged in the recovery of an unmediated presence and entirely passive when engaged in undermining it. A terminology of semi-consciousness is made to apply to the two contrary impulses: to eliminate awareness of non-presence (*conjurer*) as well as to assert it (*en contrebande*). Derrida's text does not function as if the discrimination that concerns us, namely, the mode of knowledge governing the implicit as opposed to the explicit statement, could be made in terms of the orientation of the thought (or the language) away from or toward the recouping of presence. The awareness of distance, in Rousseau, is at times stated in a blind, at times in a semi-conscious language, and the same applies to the awareness of presence. Rousseau truly seems to want it both ways, the paradox being that he wants wanting and not-wanting at the same time. This would always assume some degree of awareness, though the awareness may be directed against itself.

The "difference between an implied meaning, a nominal presence and a thematic exposition" [15] and all such distinctions within the cognitive status of language are really Rousseau's central problem, but it remains questionable whether he approached the problem explicitly or implicitly in terms of the categories of presence and distance. Derrida is brought face to face with the problem, but his terminology cannot take him any further. The structurization of Rousseau's text in terms of a presence-absence system leaves the cognitive system of deliberate knowledge versus passive knowledge unresolved and distributes it evenly on both sides.

This observation should by no means be construed as a criticism of Derrida; on the contrary. His aim is precisely to show, by a demonstration *ad absurdum,* that a crucial part of Rousseau's statement lies beyond the reach of a categorization in terms of presence and absence. On the all-important point of the cognitive status of Rousseau's language, these categories fail to function as effective indicators; Derrida's purpose in discrediting their absolute value as a base for metaphysical insight is thus achieved. Terms such as "passive," "conscious," "deliberate," etc., all of which postulate a

15. *Gr.,* p. 304. "C'est cette différence entre l'implication, la présence nominale et l'exposition thématique qui nous intéresse ici."

notion of the self as self-presence, turn out to be equally relevant or irrelevant when used on either side of the differential scale. This discredits the terms, not the author who uses them with an intent similar to that of parody: to devalue their claim to universal discriminatory power. The key to the status of Rousseau's language is not to be found in his consciousness, in his greater or lesser awareness or control over the cognitive value of his language. It can only be found in the knowledge that this language, as language, conveys about itself, thereby asserting the priority of the category of language over that of presence—which is precisely Derrida's thesis. The question remains why he postulates within Rousseau a metaphysics of presence which can then be shown not to operate, or to be dependent on the implicit power of a language which disrupts it and tears it away from its foundation. Derrida's story of Rousseau's getting, as it were, a glimpse of the truth but then going about erasing, conjuring this vision out of existence, while also surreptitiously giving in to it and smuggling it within the precinct he was assigned to protect, is undoubtedly a good story. It reverses the familiar pattern of "le brâconnier devenu garde-chasse," since it is rather the gamekeeper himself who is here doing the poaching. We should perhaps not even ask whether it is accurate, for it may well be offered as parody or fiction, without pretending to be anything else. But, unlike epistemological statements, stories do not cancel each other out, and we should not let Derrida's version replace Rousseau's own story of his involvement with language. The two stories are not quite alike and their differences are worth recording; they are instructive with regard to the cognitive status, not only of Rousseau's but also of Derrida's language and beyond that, of the language of criticism in general.

We should not be detained too long by differences in emphasis that could lead to areas of disagreement within the traditional field of Rousseau interpretation. Having deliberately bracketed the question of the author's knowledge of his own ambivalence, Derrida proceeds as if Rousseau's blindness did not require further qualification. This leads to simplifications in the description of Rousseau's stated positions on matters of ethics and history. In a

Nietzschean passage in which he claims to have freed the question of language from all ethical valorization,[16] Derrida implies a single-minded, unalterable basis for moral judgment in Rousseau —the notion of a reliable "voice" of moral consciousness—that fails to do justice to the moral intricacies of the *Nouvelle Héloïse,* or even to Derrida's own illuminating comments on the nature of pity in the *Discours sur l'origine de l'inégalité.* Having convincingly demonstrated that an arbitrary inside-outside dichotomy is used in *Essai sur l'origine des langues* to make it appear as if the hardships of distance and alienation were wrought upon man by an external catastrophical event, he makes it appear as if Rousseau understood this catastrophe in a literal sense, as an actual event in history or as the act of a personal god. Whenever a delicate transposition from the literary statement to its empirical referent occurs, Derrida seems to bypass Rousseau's complexities. Thus on the valorization of historical change or the possibility of progress, Derrida writes: "Rousseau wants to say that progress, however ambivalent, moves *either* towards deterioration, *or* toward improvement, the one or the other. . . . But Rousseau describes what he does not want to say: that progress moves in both directions, toward good and evil at the same time. This excludes eschatological and teleological endpoints, just as difference—or articulation at the source—eliminates the archeology of beginnings." [17] In fact, it would be difficult to match the rigor with which Rousseau always asserts, at the same time and at the same level of explicitness, the simultaneous movement toward progress and retrogression that Derrida here proclaims. The end of the state of nature leads to the creation of societies and their infinite possibilities of corruption—but this apparent regression is counterbalanced, at the same time, by the end of solitude and the possibility of human love. The development of reason and consciousness spells the end of tranquillity, but this tranquillity is also designated as a state of intellectual limitation similar to that of an imbecile. In such descriptions, the use of progressive and regressive terms is evenly balanced: "perfectionner la raison humaine" balances with "détériorer l'espèce," "rendre méchant" with "rendre

16. *Gr.,* p. 442.
17. *Gr.,* p. 326.

sociable." [18] The evolution of society toward inequality is far from being an unmitigated evil: we owe to it "ce qu'il y a de meilleur et de pire parmi les hommes." The end of history is seen as a relapse into a state that is undistinguishable from the state of nature, thus making the starting-point, the outcome, and the trajectory that leads from one to the other all equally ambivalent. Perhaps most typical of all is the curious movement of a long footnote to the *Discours sur l'origine de l'inégalité* in which, after having denounced with eloquence all the perils of civilization ("These are the manifest causes of all the miseries that opulence brings in the end to even the most admired of nations . . ."), Rousseau then demands from us, without any trace of irony, the utmost in civic obedience, while nevertheless despising the necessary recourse to a political order that generates its own abuses.[19] The paradoxical logic of a simultaneously positive and negative evaluation, whenever the movement of history is involved, could not be more consistent. There can be some debate as to whether the progressive and regressive movements are indeed equally balanced: in less descriptive passages, Rousseau tends to see history as a movement of decline, especially when he speaks from the point of view of the present. But whenever the double valorization occurs, the structure is simultaneous rather than alternating. Derrida's conclusion is based on an inadequate example, nor is there much evidence to be found elsewhere in Rousseau's works for such an alternating theory of historical change.[20]

None of these points is substantial. Derrida could legitimately

18. J. J. Rousseau, *Discours sur l'origine et les fondements de l'inégalité parmi les hommes* in *Oeuvres complètes,* vol. III (Ecrits politiques), Bernard Gagnebin and Marcel Raymond, eds. (Bibliothèque de la Pléiade: Paris, 1964), p. 189.
19. *Ibid.* Note IX, pp. 207–8.
20. Derrida (*Gr.,* p. 236) quotes the sentence from the *Essai sur l'origine des langues:* "La langue de convention n'appartient qu'à l'homme. Voilà pourquoi l'homme fait des progrès, soit en bien, soit en mal, et pourquoi les animaux n'en font point." Rousseau here distinguishes man from the animal in terms of historical mutability. "Soit en bien, soit en mal" indicates that the change is morally ambivalent but does not describe an alternating movement. In the *Discours sur l'économie politique* or in the second part of the *Discours sur l'origine de l'inégalité,* the dialectical movement takes place between the principles of law and freedom, on the one hand, as opposed to the necessary decline of all human political order on the other. No alternating movement of reversal from a progressive to a regressive pattern is suggested.

claim that passages in Rousseau on moral ambiguity, on the fictional (and therefore "inward") quality of the external cause for the disruption of the state of nature, on the simultaneity of historical decline and historical progress, do not in the least invalidate his reading. They are the *descriptive* passages in which Rousseau is compelled to write the reverse of what he wants to say. The same would apply to a more complex aspect of Derrida's reading: the strange economy of Rousseau's valorization of the notion of origin and the manner in which it involves him in an infinitely regressive process; he always has to substitute for the discarded origin a "deeper," more primitive state that will, in turn, have to be left behind. The same pattern appears in Derrida when he chooses to maintain a vocabulary of origin to designate the non-original quality of all so-called beginnings—as when we are told that the articulation is the origin of language, when articulation is precisely the structure that prevents all genuine origination from taking place. The use of a vocabulary of presence (or origin, nature, consciousness, etc.) to explode the claims of this vocabulary, carrying it to the logical dead-end to which it is bound to lead, is a consistent and controlled strategy throughout *De la Grammatologie*. We would be falling into a trap if we wanted to show Derrida deluded in the same manner that he claims Rousseau to be deluded. Our concern is not so much with the degree of blindness in Rousseau or in Derrida as with the rhetorical mode of their respective discourses.

It is not surprising that Derrida should be more detailed and eloquent in expounding the philosophy of written language and of "difference" that Rousseau rejects than in expounding the philosophy of plenitude that Rousseau wants to defend. He has, after all, a massive tradition of Rousseau interpretation behind him to support his view of him as an avowed philosopher of unmediated presence. In this respect, his image of Rousseau is so traditional that it hardly needs to be restated. The main bulk of his analysis therefore deals with the gradual chipping away of Rousseau's theory of presence under the onus of his own language. On at least two points, however, Derrida goes out of his way to demonstrate the strict orthodoxy of Rousseau's position with regard to the traditional ontology of Western thought, and in at least one of these instances, he can do so only at the expense of a considerable and original interpretative effort that has to move well beyond and even against the face-value of Rousseau's own statement.[21] Significantly, the two passages have to do with Rousseau's use and understanding of rhetorical figures. On the questions of nature, of self, of origin, even of morality, Derrida starts out from the current view in Rousseau interpretation and then proceeds to show how Rousseau's own text undermines his declared philosophical allegiances. But on the two points involving rhetoric, Derrida goes the tradition one better. It is obviously important for him that Rousseau's theory and practice of rhetoric would also fall under the imperatives of what he calls a "logocentric" ontology that privileges the spoken word over the written word. This is also the point at which we have to reverse the interpretative process and start reading Derrida in terms of Rousseau rather than vice versa.

The two closely related rhetorical figures discussed by Derrida, both prominently in evidence in the *Essai sur l'origine des langues*, are imitation (mimesis) and metaphor. In order to demonstrate the logocentric orthodoxy of Rousseau's theory of metaphor, Derrida has to show that his conception of representation is based on an imitation in which the ontological status of the imitated entity is not put into question. Representation is an ambivalent process that implies the absence of what is being made present again, and this absence cannot be assumed to be merely contingent. However, when representation is conceived as imitation, in the classical sense of eighteenth-century aesthetic theory, it confirms rather than undermines the plenitude of the represented entity. It functions as a mnemotechnic sign that brings back something that happened not to be there at the moment, but whose existence in another place, at another time, or in a different mode of consciousness is not challenged. The model for this idea of representation is the painted image, restoring the object to view as if it were present and thus assuring the continuation of its presence. The power of the image reaches beyond duplication of sense data: the mimetic imagination is able to convert non-sensory, "inward" patterns of ex-

21. I am referring to the passage on metaphor (*Gr.*, pp. 381–97) here discussed on pp. 133–35.

perience (feelings, emotions, passions) into objects of perception and can therefore represent as actual, concrete presences, experiences of consciousness devoid of objective existence. This possibility is often stressed as the main function of non-representational art forms such as music: they imitate by means of signs linked by natural right with the emotions which they signify. A representative eighteenth-century aesthetician, the abbé Du Bos, writes:

> Just as the painter imitates the lines and colors of nature, the musician imitates the tone, the stresses, the pauses, the voice-inflections, in short all the sounds by means of which nature itself expresses its feelings and emotions. All these sounds . . . are powerfully effective in conveying emotions, because they are the signs of passion instituted by nature itself. They receive their strength directly from nature, whereas articulated words are merely the arbitrary signs of the passions. . . . Music groups the natural signs of the passions and uses them artfully to increase the power of the words it makes into song. These natural signs have an amazing power in awakening emotions in those who hear them. They receive this power from nature itself.[22]

Classical eighteenth-century theories of representation persistently strive to reduce music and poetry to the status of painting.[23] "La musique peint les passions" and *ut pictura poesis* are the great commonplaces of an aesthetic creed that involves its proponents in an interesting maze of problems, without, however, leading them to revise their premises. The possibility of making the invisible visible, of giving presence to what can only be imagined, is repeatedly stated as the main function of art. The stress on subject-matter as the basis for aesthetic judgment stems from such a creed. It involves the representation of what lies beyond the senses as a means to confer upon it the ontological stability of perceived objects. One is interested in the subject-matter primarily because it

22. Jean Baptiste (abbé) Du Bos, *Réflexions critiques sur la poésie et sur la peinture* (Paris, 1740) vol. I, pp. 435–36, 438.
23. *Ibid.* "Il n'y a de la vérité dans une symphonie, composée pour imiter une tempête, que lorsque le chant de la symphonie, son harmonie et son rhythme nous font entendre un bruit pareil au fracas que les vents font dans l'air et au mugissement des flots qui s'entrechoquent, ou qui se brisent contre les rochers." (Du Bos, *op. cit.* p. 440.)

confirms that the unseen can be represented: representation is the condition that confirms the possibility of imitation as universal proof of presence. The need for the reassurance of such a proof stands behind many characteristic statements of the period [24] and confirms its orthodoxy in terms of a metaphysics of presence.

At first sight, Rousseau seems to continue the tradition, specifically in the passages from the *Essai* that deal with the characterization of music and that differ little from the classical statements of his predecessors. His stress on the inwardness of music is entirely compatible with his proclaimed theory of music as imitation: "The sounds in a melody do not only affect us as sounds, but as signs of our emotions, of our feelings. This is how they produce within us the responses they express and how we recognize the image of our emotions in them." [25] From the point of view of imitation, there is no difference between the outward physical impressions and the "impressions morales." "Passions" and "objets" can be used interchangeably without modifying the nature of imitation.

> Beautiful, well-shaded colors please our sight, but this pleasure is purely of the senses. Colors come to life and move us because of the design (le dessin), the imitation. We are affected by the objects represented and by the passions expressed in the design of the painting. The interest and the seductiveness of the picture does not stem from the colors. We will still be moved by the outline (les traits) of a painting that has been

24. The following passage from Du Bos is a typical example: "Un peintre peut donc passer pour un grand artisan, en qualité de dessinateur élégant ou de coloriste rival de la nature, quand même il ne saurait pas faire usage de ses talents pour représenter des objets touchants, et pour mettre dans ses tableaux l'âme et la vraisemblance qui se font sentir dans ceux de Raphaël et du Poussin. Les tableaux de l'école Lombarde sont admirés, bien que les peintres s'y soient bornés souvent à flatter les yeux par la richesse et par la vérité de leurs couleurs, sans penser peut-être que l'art fut capable de nous attendrir: mais leurs partisans les plus zélés tombent d'accord qu'il manque une grande beauté aux tableaux de cette école, et que ceux du Titien, par exemple, seraient encore bien plus précieux s'il avait traité toujours de sujets touchants, et s'il eut joint plus souvent les talents de son Ecole aux talents de l'Ecole romaine." (Du Bos, *op. cit.* p. 69.)

25. J. J. Rousseau, *Essai sur l'origine des langues,* texte reproduit d'après l'édition A. Belin de 1817 (Bibliothèque du Graphe: Paris, n.d.), p. 534. Henceforth designated as *Essai.*

reduced to a print but, if we remove the outline, the colors will lose all their power.

Melody does for music exactly what design does for painting. . . .[26]

Derrida seems altogether justified in seeing Rousseau as a traditional expounder of a theory of imitation that bridges the distinction between external and inward themes.

> Rousseau remains faithful to a tradition that is unaffected by his thought: he stays convinced that the essence of art is imitation (*mimesis*). Imitation duplicates presence: it is added to the presence of the entity which it replaces. It transposes what is present into an "outside" version of this presence (elle fait donc passer le présent dans son dehors). In the inanimate arts, the "outside" version of the entity is being duplicated: we have the "outside" reproduction of an "outside" version (la reproduction du dehors dans le dehors). . . . In animate art, most emphatically in song, the "outside" imitates an "inside" (le dehors imite le dedans). It is *expressive*. It "paints" the passions. The metaphor that transforms song into painting can force the inwardness of its power into the outwardness of space only under the aegis of the concept of imitation, shared alike by music and by painting. Whatever their differences, music and painting both are duplications, representations. Both equally partake of the categories of outside and inside. The expression has already begun to move the passion outside itself into the open and has already begun to paint it.[27]

The rest of Derrida's analysis will then show how imitation, which expresses an avowed desire for presence, surreptitiously functions, in Rousseau's text, as the undoing of a desire that it reduces to absurdity by its very existence: there never would be a need for imitation if the presence had not been *a priori* preempted (entamée).

Turning with this reading in mind to the section of the *Essai* that deals with music, we find something different, especially if we take into account some of the passages that Derrida does not

26. *Essai*, pp. 530–31.
27. *Gr.*, pp. 289–90.

include in his commentary.* In Chapters XIII to XVI of the *Essai,* Rousseau is not so much bent on showing that music, painting and art in general do not involve sensation (as seems to be the thrust of his polemical argument against sensualist aesthetics), but that the sensory element that is necessarily a part of the pictorial or musical sign plays no part in the aesthetic experience. Hence the priority of drawing (le trait, le dessin) over color, of melody over sound, because both are oriented toward meaning and less dependent on seductive sensory impressions. Like Du Bos, Rousseau seems eager to safeguard the importance of subject matter (or, in the case of literature, of meaning) over the sign. When he pays attention, at moments, to the sign, as in the statement: "Les couleurs et les sons peuvent beaucoup comme représentation et signes, peu de chose comme simples objets de sens," [28] this does not imply any willingness to dissociate the sign from the sensation or to state its autonomy. The sign never ceases to function as *signifiant* and remains entirely oriented toward a meaning.[29] Its own sensory component is contingent and distracting. The reason for this, however, is not, as Derrida suggests, because Rousseau wants the meaning of the sign, the *signifié,* to exist as plenitude and as presence. The sign is devoid of substance, not because it has to be a transparent indicator that should not mask a plenitude of meaning, but because the meaning itself is empty; the sign should not offer its own sensory richness as a substitute for the void that it signifies. Contrary to Derrida's assertion, Rousseau's theory of representation is not directed toward meaning as presence and plenitude but toward meaning as void.

The movement of the sixteenth chapter of the *Essai,* entitled, "Fausse analogie entre les couleurs et les sons" bears this out. Reversing the prevailing hierarchy of eighteenth-century aesthetic theory, it states the priority of music over painting (and, within music, of melody over harmony) in terms of a value-system that is structural rather than substantial: music is called superior to

* With perfect right, within the logic of his own argument, which would consider these passages as redundant or dealt with elsewhere in the commentary. The validity of my emphasis has to stand on its own merits and be responsible for it own omissions, not less blatant than Derrida's for being different.
28. *Essai,* p. 535.
29. As stated by Derrida, *Gr.,* p. 296.

painting despite and even because of its lack of substance. With remarkable foresight, Rousseau describes music as a pure system of relations that at no point depends on the substantive assertions of a presence, be it as a sensation or as a consciousness. Music is a mere play of relationships:

> . . . for us, each sound is a relative entity. No sound by itself possesses absolute attributes that allow us to identify it: it is high or low, loud or soft with respect to another sound only. By itself, it has none of these properties. In a harmonic system, a given sound is nothing by natural right (un son quelconque n'est *rien* non plus *naturellement*). It is neither tonic, nor dominant, harmonic or fundamental. All these properties exist as relationships only and since the entire system can vary from bass to treble, each sound changes in rank and place as the system changes in degree.[30]

"Un son n'est rien . . . naturellement." Are we entitled to italicize and isolate this passage as proof of the negation of the substantiality of meaning in Rousseau? Not on the basis of the sentence just quoted, but with greater semblance of truth if we take the neighboring passages into account, for it seems that Rousseau fully understood the implications and consequences of what he was saying. Music is not reduced to a system of relationships because it functions as a mere structure of sounds independently of meaning, or because it is able to obscure the meaning by seducing the senses. There is no vacillation in Rousseau as to the semiotic and non-sensory status of the sign. Music becomes a mere structure because it is hollow at the core, because it "means" the negation of all presence. It follows that the musical structure obeys an entirely different principle from that of structures resting on a "full" sign, regardless of whether the sign refers to sensation or to a state of consciousness. Not being grounded in any substance, the musical sign can never have any assurance of existence. It can never be identical with itself or with prospective repetitions of itself, even if these future sounds possess the same physical properties of pitch and timbre as the present one. The identities of physics have no bearing on the mode of

30. *Essai,* p. 536.

being of a sign that is, by definition, unaffected by sensory attributes. "Colors remain but sounds faint away and we can never be certain that the sounds reborn are the same as the sounds that vanished." [31]

Unlike the stable, synchronic sensation of "painting," [32] music can never rest for a moment in the stability of its own existence: it steadily has to repeat itself in a movement that is bound to remain endless. This movement persists regardless of any illusion of presence, regardless of the manner in which the subject interprets its intentionality: it is determined by the nature of sign as *signifiant*, by the nature of music as language. The resulting repetitive pattern is the ground of temporality: "The field of music is time, that of painting space." The duration of the colors, in painting, is spatial and constitutes therefore a misleading analogy for the necessarily diachronic structure of music. On the one hand, music is condemned to exist always as a moment, as a persistently frustrated intent toward meaning; on the other hand, this very frustration prevents it from remaining within the moment. Musical signs are unable to coincide: their dynamics are always oriented toward the future of their repetition, never toward the consonance of their simultaneity. Even the apparent harmony of the single sound, *à l'unisson*, has to spread itself out into a pattern of successive repetition; considered as a musical sign, the single sound is in fact the melody of its potential repetition. "Nature does not analyze [sound] into its harmonic components: it hides them instead under the illusion of unison (l'apparence de l'unisson). . . ."

Music is the diachronic version of the pattern of non-coincidence within the moment. Rousseau attributes to nature the imaginative power to create melody when it refers to noises such as the song of the birds, but it becomes distinctively human in reference to music: ". . . if nature sometimes breaks down [the song into its harmonic components] in the modulated song of man

31. *Ibid.* p. 536.
32. "Painting" here designates the general prejudice in favor of the image as presence in eighteenth-century aesthetics. It goes without saying that when painting is conceived as art, the illusion of plenitude can be undermined in the plastic arts as well as in poetry or music; the problem, as is well known, figures prominently in contemporary discussions about non-representational painting.

or in the song of birds, it does so sequentially, putting one sound after the other: it inspires song, not chords; it dictates melody, not harmony." [33] Harmony is rejected as a mistaken illusion of consonance within the necessarily dissonant structure of the moment. Melody does not partake of this mystification: it does not offer a resolution of the dissonance but its projection on a temporal, diachronic axis.

The successive structure of music is therefore the direct consequence of its non-mimetic character. Music does not imitate, for its referent is the negation of its very substance, the sound. Rousseau states this in a remarkable sentence that Derrida does not quote: "It is one of the main privileges of the musician to be able to paint things that are inaudible, whereas the painter cannot represent things that are invisible. An art that operates entirely by means of motion can accomplish the amazing feat of conveying the very image of repose. Sleep, the quiet of night, solitude and even silence can enter into the picture that music paints. . . ." [34] The sentence starts off by reaffirming that music is capable of imitating the most inward, invisible, and inaudible of feelings; the use of the pictorial vocabulary suggests that we have re-entered the orthodoxy of eighteenth-century representational theory. But as the enumeration proceeds, the content of the sentiment which, in Du Bos, was rich in all the plenitude and interest of experience, is increasingly hollowed out, emptied of all trace of substance. The idyllic overtones of tranquillity tend to disappear if one remembers to what extent music itself depends on motion; the "repos" should also be understood negatively as loss

___

33. *Essai*, p. 536. See also, p. 537: "les oiseaux sifflent, l'homme seul chante. . . ."

34. *Ibid.* p. 537. Cf. the passage on silence in Du Bos, *op. cit.* pp. 447–48. Rousseau's allusion to "une lecture égale et monotone à laquelle on s'endort" parallels Du Bos: "Un homme qui parle longtemps sur le même ton, endort les autres . . .", possibly suggesting a direct echo in Rousseau, certainly a very similar point of departure. But Rousseau does not simply refer to a mechanical effect that would allow for a musical "imitation" of silence: he distinguishes at once between this automatic action and a much closer affinity between music and silence: "la musique agit plus intimement sur nous. . . ." The rest of the paragraph complicates matters further by bringing in notions of irreversible synaesthesia between music and painting, but does not pursue the paradox of a "music of silence" that has just been stated.

of motion and therefore as a restatement of the inherent fragility, impermanence, and self-destructiveness of music. The solitude is equally disquieting since much has been made elsewhere in the text of music as the element that sets man apart from nature and unites him with other men. And the radically paradoxical formulation that the musical sign can refer to silence would have for its equivalent, in the other arts, that painting refers to the absence of all light and color, and that language refers to the absence of meaning.[35] The passage prefigures its later, more extreme version in *La Nouvelle Héloïse*: "tel est le néant des choses humaines qu'hors l'Etre existant par lui-même, il n'y a rien de beau que ce qui n'est pas." [36]

It would not be fruitful to dispute these statements on the basis of a different phenomenology of music: the avowed thesis of the *Essai* equates music with language and makes it clear that, throughout the text, Rousseau never ceased to speak about the nature of language. What is here called language, however, differs entirely from an instrumental means of communication: for that purpose, a mere gesture, a mere cry would suffice. Rousseau acknowledges the existence of language from the moment speech is structured according to a principle similar to that of music. Like music, language is a diachronic system of relationships, the succesive sequence of a *narrative*. "The sequential effect of discourse, as it repeats its point again and again, conveys a much stronger emotion than the presence of the object itself, where the full meaning is revealed in one single stroke. Let us assume that we confront a familiar situation of grief. The sight of the bereaved person will hardly move us to tears, but if we give him time to tell all that he feels, our tears will soon begin to flow." [37] The structural characteristics of language are exactly the same as those attributed to music: the misleading synchronism of the visual perception which creates a false illusion of presence has to be replaced by a succession of discontinuous moments that

35. "Musicienne du silence . . ." is a famous line from Mallarmé ("Sainte"). It could be argued that Mallarmé went less far than Rousseau in seeing the implications of this line for a representational theory of poetry.
36. Rousseau, *La Nouvelle Héloïse*, Pléiade edition, *Oeuvres complètes*, vol. II, p. 693.
37. *Essai*, p. 503.

create the fiction of a repetitive temporality. That this diachrony is indeed a fiction, that it belongs to the language of writing and of art and not to a language of needs is made clear by the choice of an example taken, not from life, but from a dramatic perform-ance: "Scenes from a tragedy reach their effect [by sequential dis-course] only. Mere pantomime without words will leave us nearly cold, but speech even without gestures will make us weep." [38] All sequential language is dramatic, narrative language. It is also the language of passion because passion, in Rousseau, is precisely the manifestation of a will that exists independently of any specific meaning or intent and that therefore can never be traced back to a cause or origin. "A man will weep at the sight of a tragic per-formance even though he never felt pity for a person in need." [39] But pity, the arch passion in Rousseau is itself, as Derrida has very well perceived, inherently a fictional process that transposes an actual situation into a world of appearance, of drama and literary language: all pity is in essence theatrical. It follows that the diachronic pattern of narrative discourse, which confers upon this discourse the semblance of a beginning, of a continuity, and of an ending, by no means implies a quest for origin, not even the metaphorical representation of such a quest. Neither the *Discours sur l'origine de l'inégalité* nor the *Essai sur l'origine des langues* is the history of a genetic movement, of an organic process of birth and decay: Rousseau's famous statement "Commençons donc par écarter tous les faits . . ." cannot be taken too radically and applies to the mode of language used throughout the two texts. They do not "represent" a successive event, but are the melodic, musical, successive projection of a single moment of radical contradiction—the present—upon the temporal axis of a diachronic narrative. The only point at which they touch upon an empirical reality is in their common rejection of any present as totally intolerable and devoid of meaning.[40] Diachronic structures such as music, melody, or allegory are favored over pseudo-syn-

38. *Ibid.* p. 503.
39. *Ibid.* p. 503 (Rousseau's own footnote).
40. Clearly stated in the last chapter of the *Essai* entitled "Rapport des langues aux gouvernements," the true point of departure of the text. The same applies, in a somewhat more diffuse way, to the *Discours sur l'origine de l'inégalité.*

chronic structures such as painting, harmony, or mimesis because the latter mislead one into believing in a stability of meaning that does not exist. The elegiac tone that is occasionally sounded does not express a nostalgia for an original presence but is a purely dramatic device, an effect made possible and dictated by a fiction that deprives the nostalgia of all foundation.[41] It does not suffice to say that, in these texts, origin is merely a metaphor that "stands for" a beginning, even if one makes it clear that Rousseau's theory of figural language breaks with any idea of representation. The origin here "precedes" the present for purely structural and not chronological reasons. Chronology is the structural correlative of the necessarily figural nature of literary language.

It is in that sense that the title of the third chapter of the *Essai* must be understood: "Que le premier langage dut être figuré." The only literal statement that says what it means to say is the assertion that there can be no literal statements. In the narrative rhetoric of Rousseau's text, this is what is meant by the chronological fiction that the "first" language had to be poetic language. Derrida, who sees Rousseau as a representational writer, has to show instead that his theory of metaphor is founded on the priority of the literal over the metaphorical meaning, of the "sens propre" over the "sens figuré." And since Rousseau explicitly says the opposite, Derrida has to interpret the chapter on metaphor as a moment of blindness in which Rousseau says the opposite of what he means to say.

The argument on this point duplicates the line of reasoning applied to representation: Rousseau no longer locates the literal meaning in the referent of the metaphor as an object, but he interiorizes the object and makes the metaphor refer to an inner state of consciousness, a feeling or a passion. "Rousseau bestows upon the expression of emotions a literal meaning that he is willing to relinquish, from the start, in the designation of objects."[42] In accordance with Derrida's general image of Rous-

---

41. The point should be developed in terms of the *Discours sur l'origine de l'inégalité,* showing that elegiac passages are associated with a deluded primitivism unequivocally condemned in the text as a whole. (See, for example, the section on p. 133 beginning "Les temps dont je vais parler sont bien éloignés. . . .")

42. *Gr.,* p. 389.

seau's place in the history of Western thought—the moment when the postulate of presence is taken out of the external world and transposed within the self-reflective inwardness of a consciousness—the recovery of presence is shown to occur along the axis of an inner-outer polarity. Derrida can use Rousseau's own example of metaphor to prove his case: the primitive man who designates the first other men he encounters by the term "giants," blindly coins a metaphorical term to state a literal meaning, the inner experience of fear. The statement, "I see a giant" is a metaphor for the literal statement, "I am frightened," a feeling that could not be expressed by saying, "I see a man (like myself)." Rousseau uses this example to indicate that the transposed meaning can "precede" the literal one. But the example is badly chosen, possibly, as Derrida suggests,[43] under the influence of Condillac, to whose *Essai sur l'origine des connaissances humaines* Rousseau is alluding in the chapter on metaphor. The "babes in the woods" topos is used by Condillac to make language originate out of a feeling of fear.[44] In Rousseau's vocabulary, language is a product of passion and not the expression of a need; fear, the reverse side of violence and agression, is distinctively utilitarian and belongs to the world of "besoins" rather than "passions." Fear would hardly need language and would be best expressed by pantomime, by mere gesture. All passion is to some degree *passion inutile,* made gratuitous by the non-existence of an object or a cause. The possibility of passion distinguishes man from the animal: "The need for subsistence forces man apart from other men, but the passions draw them together. The first speech was not caused by hunger or thirst, but by love, hatred, pity and anger."[45] Fear is

---

43. *Ibid.* p. 393. The argument on the same page in which Derrida tries to show the priority of fear over pity as the "earlier" passion, loses what was gained by the masterful insight in the nature of pity as an element of distance and difference (*Gr.,* p. 262). The distinction between "passion" and "besoin" cannot be made in terms of origin but of substance: the substantial referent of the need is missing in the case of the passion.

44. Condillac, *Essai sur l'origine des connaissances humaines,* Part II, Section I (De l'origine et des progrès du langage): "Celui [des deux enfants abandonnés dans le désert] qui voyait un lieu où il avait été effrayé, imitait les cris et les mouvements qui étaient les signes de la frayeur, pour avertir l'autre de ne pas s'exposer au danger qu'il avait connu." *Oeuvres* (Paris, 1798), vol. I, p. 263.

45. *Gr.,* p. 505.

on the side of hunger and thirst and could never, by itself, lead to the supplementary figuration of language; it is much too practical to be called a passion. The third chapter of the *Essai*, the section on metaphor, should have been centered on pity, or its extension: love (or hate). When the story of the "birth" of figural language is told later in the text (Chapter IX, p. 525) it is directly associated with love, not with fear. The definitive statement, here again, is to be found in the *Nouvelle Héloïse*: "Love is mere illusion. It invents, so to speak, another universe; it surrounds itself with objects that do not exist or to which only love itself has given life. Since it expresses all its feelings by means of images it speaks only in figures (comme il rend tous ses sentiments en images, son langage est toujours figuré)." [46] The metaphorical language which, in the fictional diachrony of the *Essai*, is called "premier" has no literal referent. Its only referent is "le néant des choses humaines."

Although—with regard to his own as well as to Derrida's main statement on the nature of language—Rousseau's theory of rhetoric is peripheral, it is not unimportant within the narrow context of our own question, which deals with the cognitive structure of the interpretative process. To extend the argument to other areas of assent and disagreement with Derrida, would be tedious and unnecessary. On the question of rhetoric, on the nature of figural language, Rousseau was not deluded and said what he meant to say. And it is equally significant that, precisely on this same point, his best modern interpreter had to go out of his way *not* to understand him. The *Discours sur l'origine de l'inégalité* and the *Essai sur l'origine des langues* are texts whose discursive assertions account for their rhetorical mode. What is being said about the nature of language makes it unavoidable that the texts should be written in the form of a fictionally diachronic narrative or, if one prefers to call it so, of an allegory. [47] The allegorical mode is accounted for in the description of all language as figural and in the necessarily diachronic structure of the reflection that reveals this insight.

46. Rousseau, *La Nouvelle Héloïse*, Pléiade edition, vol. II, p. 15.
47. For another preparatory statement on allegory in Rousseau, see Paul de Man, "The Rhetoric of Temporality" in *Interpretation: Theory and Practise*, Charles Singleton, ed. (Johns Hopkins Press, 1969), pp. 184–88.

The text goes beyond this, however, for as it accounts for its own mode of writing, it states at the same time the necessity of making this statement itself in an indirect, figural way that knows it will be misunderstood by being taken literally. Accounting for the "rhetoricity" of its own mode, the text also postulates the necessity of its own misreading. It knows and asserts that it will be misunderstood. It tells the story, the allegory of its misunderstanding: the necessary degradation of melody into harmony, of language into painting, of the language of passion into the language of need, of metaphor into literal meaning. In accordance with its own language, it can only tell this story as a fiction, knowing full well that the fiction will be taken for fact and the fact for fiction; such is the necessarily ambivalent nature of literary language. Rousseau's own language, however, is not blind to this ambivalence: proof of this lies in the entire organization of his discourse and more explicit in what it says about representation and metaphor as the cornerstone of a theory of rhetoric. The consistency of a rhetoric that can assert itself only in a manner that leaves open the possibility of misunderstanding, adds further proof. The rhetorical character of literary language opens up the possibility of the archetypal error: the recurrent confusion of sign and substance. That Rousseau was misunderstood confirms his own theory of misunderstanding. Derrida's version of this misunderstanding comes closer than any previous version to Rousseau's actual statement because it singles out as the point of maximum blindness the area of greatest lucidity: the theory of rhetoric and its inevitable consequences.

How then does Derrida's text differ from Rousseau's? We are entitled to generalize in working our way toward a definition by giving Rousseau exemplary value and calling "literary," in the full sense of the term, any text that implicitly or explicitly signifies its own rhetorical mode and prefigures its own misunderstanding as the correlative of its rhetorical nature; that is, of its "rhetoricity." It can do so by declarative statement or by poetic inference.[48] "To

48. A discursive, critical, or philosophical text that does this by means of statements is therefore not more or less literary than a poetic text that would avoid direct statement. In practice, the distinctions are often blurred: the logic of many philosophical texts relies heavily on narrative coherence and figures of speech,

account for" or "to signify," in the sentence above, does not designate a subjective process: it follows from the rhetorical nature of
literary language that the cognitive function resides in the language and not in the subject. The question as to whether the
author himself is or is not blinded is to some extent irrelevant;
it can only be asked heuristically, as a means to accede to the
true question: whether his language is or is not blind to its
own statement. By asking this question of *De la Grammatologie*,
a way back can be found to the starting-point of the inquiry:
the interplay between critical and literary language in terms of
blindness and insight.

It would seem to matter very little whether Derrida is right
or wrong about Rousseau, since his own text resembles the *Essai*
so closely, in its rhetoric as well as in its statement. It also tells a
story: the repression of written language by what is here called
the "logocentric" fallacy of favoring voice over writing is narrated
as a consecutive, historical process. Throughout, Derrida uses
Heidegger's and Nietzsche's fiction of metaphysics as a *period* in
Western thought in order to dramatize, to give tension and
suspense to the argument, exactly as Rousseau gave tension and
suspense to the story of language and of society by making them
pseudo-historical. Neither is Derrida taken in by the theatricality
of his gesture or the fiction of his narrative: exactly as Rousseau
tells us obliquely, but consistently, that we are reading a fiction
and not a history. Derrida's Nietzschean theory of language as
"play" warns us not to take him literally, especially when his
statements seem to refer to concrete historical situations such as
the present. The use of a philosophical terminology with the
avowed purpose of discrediting this very terminology is an established philosophical procedure that has many antecedents besides
Rousseau and is one that Derrida practices with exemplary skill.
Finally, Derrida's theory of *écriture* corresponds closely to Rousseau's statement on the figural nature of the language of passion.
Does it matter then whether we attribute the final statement to
Rousseau or to Derrida since both are in fact saying the same

---

while poetry abounds in general statements. The criterion of literary specificity
does not depend on the greater or lesser discursiveness of the mode but on the
degree of consistent "rhetoricity" of the language.

BLINDNESS AND INSIGHT

thing? Of course, if Rousseau does not belong to the logocentric "period," then the scheme of periodization used by Derrida is avowedly arbitrary.[49] If we argue, moreover, that Rousseau escapes from the logocentric fallacy precisely to the extent that his language *is literary*, then we are saying by implication that the myth of the priority of oral language over written language has always already been demystified by literature, although literature remains persistently open to being misunderstood for doing the opposite. None of this seems to be inconsistent with Derrida's insight, but it might distress some of his more literal-minded followers: his historical scheme is merely a narrative convention and the brief passage on the nature of literary language in *De la Grammatologie* seems to tend in the direction suggested. Nevertheless, although Derrida can be "right" on the nature of literary language and consistent in the application of this insight to his own text, he remains unwilling or unable to read Rousseau as literature. Why does he have to reproach Rousseau for doing exactly what he legitimately does himself? According to Derrida, Rousseau's rejection of a logocentric theory of language, which the author of the *Essai* encounters in the guise of the aesthetic sensualism of the eighteenth century, "could not be a radical rejection, for it occurs within the framework inherited from this philosophy and of the 'metaphysical' conception of art."[50] I have tried to show instead that Rousseau's use of a traditional vocabulary is exactly similar, in its strategy and its implications, to the use Derrida consciously makes of the traditional vocabulary of Western philosophy. What happens in Rousseau is exactly what happens in Derrida: a vocabulary of substance and of presence is no longer used declaratively but rhetorically, for the very reasons that are being (metaphor-

49. It is an open question whether Derrida would be willing to accept all the consequences of such a change in historical periodization—such as, for example, the possibility of an entirely affirmative answer to the question asked with reference to Lévi-Strauss: "Accorder en soi Rousseau, Marx et Freud est une tâche difficile. Les accorder entre eux, dans la rigueur systématique du concept, est-ce possible?" (*Gr.*, p. 173).
50. *Gr.*, p. 297. "Metaphysical" here means, in Heidegger's post-Nietzschean terminology, the era during which the ontological difference between being and entity (Sein und Seiendes) remains implicit (ungedacht). Derrida radicalizes the ontological difference by locating the differential tension within language, between language as voice and language as sign.

ically) stated. Rousseau's text has no blind spots:[51] it accounts at all moments for its own rhetorical mode. Derrida misconstrues as blindness what is instead a transposition from the literal to the figural level of discourse.

There are two possible explanations for Derrida's blindness with regard to Rousseau: either he actually misreads Rousseau, possibly because he substitutes Rousseau's interpreters for the author himself—maybe whenever Derrida writes "Rousseau," we should read "Starobinski" or "Raymond" or "Poulet"—or he deliberately misreads Rousseau for the sake of his own exposition and rhetoric. In the first case, Derrida's blindness merely confirms Rousseau's foreknowledge of the misinterpretation of his work. It would be a classical case of critical blindness, somewhat different in aspect but not in essence from the pattern encountered in critics such as Lukács, Poulet, or Blanchot. Their blindness, it will be remembered, consisted in the affirmation of a methodology that could be "deconstructed" in terms of their own findings: Poulet's "self" turns out to be language, Blanchot's impersonality a metaphor for self-reading, etc.; in all these cases, the methodological dogma is being played off against the literary insight, and this interplay between methodology and literature develops in turn the highly literary rhetoric of what could be called systematic criticism. Derrida's case is somewhat different: his chapter on method, on literary interpretation as deconstruction, is flawless in itself but made to apply to the wrong object. There is no need to deconstruct Rousseau; the established tradition of Rousseau interpretation, however, stands in dire need of deconstruction. Derrida found himself in the most favorable of all critical positions: he was dealing with an author as clear-sighted as language lets him be who, for that very reason, is being systematically misread; the author's own works, newly interpreted, can then be played off against the most talented of his deluded interpreters or followers. Needless to say, this new interpretation will, in its turn, be caught in its own form of blindness, but not without having produced its own bright moment of literary insight. Derrida did not choose to adopt this pattern: instead of having Rousseau deconstruct his critics, we

51. The choice of the wrong example to illustrate metaphor (fear instead of pity) is a mistake, not a blind spot.

have Derrida deconstructing a pseudo-Rousseau by means of insights that could have been gained from the "real" Rousseau. The pattern is too interesting not to be deliberate.

At any rate, the pattern accounts very well for the slight thematic difference between Derrida's story and Rousseau's story. Whereas Rousseau tells the story of an inexorable regression, Derrida rectifies a recurrent error of judgment. His text, as he puts it so well, is the unmaking of a construct. However negative it may sound, deconstruction implies the possibility of rebuilding. Derrida's dialectical energy, especially in the first half of his book, which does not deal directly with Rousseau, clearly gains its momentum from the movement of deconstruction that takes place in the second part, using Rousseau as a sparring partner. Rousseau plays for Derrida somewhat the same part that Wagner plays for Nietzsche in *The Birth of Tragedy*, a text *De la Grammatologie* resembles even more closely than it resembles the *Essai sur l'origine des langues*. The fact that Wagner serves a presumptively positive function in Nietzsche, whereas Rousseau is an antithetical mask or shadow for Derrida, matters very little: the type of mis-reading is very similar in both cases. Rousseau needed no equiva-lent mediating figure in the *Essai*; he takes his energy entirely from the strength of his radical rejection of the present moment. The attacks on Rameau, on Condillac, on Du Bos or the tradition Du Bos represents, are contingent polemics not an essential part of the structure: what stands under indictment is language itself and not somebody's philosophical error. Neither does Rousseau hold up any hope that one could ever escape from the regressive process of misunderstanding that he describes; he cuts himself off once and forever from all future disciples. In this respect, Derrida's text is less radical, less mature than Rousseau's, though not less literary. Nor is it less important from a philosophical point of view than *The Birth of Tragedy*. As is well known, Nietzsche himself later criticized the use he had made of Wagner in the early book, not merely because he changed his mind about the latter's merits—he had, in fact, already lost most of his illusions about Wagner when he wrote *The Birth of Tragedy*—but because his presence in that text stood in the way of the musicality, the allegory of its mode: "Sie hätte singen sollen, diese 'neue Seele'— und nicht reden"—"it should have sung, this 'new soul,' and not have spoken." He went on to write *Zarathustra* and *Will to Power*, and one may wonder if he was ever able to free himself entirely from Wagner: it may be that an all too hopeful future was converted into an all too aberrant past. Rousseau went on to write a "pure" fiction, *La Nouvelle Héloïse*, and a treatise of constitutional law, *Le Contrat social*—but that is another story, as is the future of Jacques Derrida's own work.

The critical reading of Derrida's critical reading of Rousseau shows blindness to be the necessary correlative of the rhetorical nature of literary language. Within the structure of the system: text-reader-critic (in which the critic can be defined as the "second" reader or reading) the moment of blindness can be located differently. If the literary text itself has areas of blindness, the system can be binary; reader and critic coincide in their attempt to make the unseen visible. Our reading of some literary critics, in this volume, is a special, somewhat more complex case of this structure: the literary texts are themselves critical but blinded, and the critical reading of the critics tries to deconstruct the blindness. It should be clear by now that "blindness" implies no literary value-judgment: Lukács, Blanchot, Poulet, and Derrida can be called "literary," in the full sense of the term, because of their blindness, not in spite of it. In the more complicated case of the non-blinded author—as we have claimed Rousseau to be—the system has to be triadic: the blindness is transferred from the writer to his first readers, the "traditional" disciples or commentators. These blinded first readers—they could be replaced for the sake of exposition, by the fiction of a naïve reader, though the tradition is likely to provide ample material—then need, in turn, a critical reader who reverses the tradition and momentarily takes us closer to the original insight. The existence of a particularly rich aberrant tradition in the case of the writers who can legitimately be called the most enlightened, is therefore no accident, but a constitutive part of all literature, the basis, in fact, of literary history. And since interpretation is nothing but the possibility of error, by claiming that a certain degree of blindness is part of the specificity of all literature we also reaffirm the absolute dependence of the interpretation on the text and of the text on the interpretation.

VIII

Literary History and Literary Modernity

To write reflectively about modernity leads to problems that put the usefullness of the term into question, especially as it applies, or fails to apply, to literature. There may well be an inherent contradiction between modernity, which is a way of acting and behaving, and such terms as "reflection" or "ideas" that play an important part in literature and history. The spontaneity of being modern conflicts with the claim to think and write about modernity; it is not at all certain that literature and modernity are in any way compatible concepts. Yet we all speak readily about modern literature and even use this term as a device for historical periodization, with the same apparent unawareness that history and modernity may well be even more incompatible than literature and modernity. The innocuous-sounding title of this essay may therefore contain no less than two logical absurdities—a most inauspicious beginning.

The term "modernity" reappears with increasing frequency and seems again to have become an issue not only as an ideological weapon, but as a theoretical problem as well. It may even be one of the ways by means of which the link between literary theory and literary praxis is being partly restored. At other moments in history, the topic "modernity" might be used just as an attempt at self-definition, as a way of diagnosing one's own present. This can happen during periods of considerable inventiveness, periods that seem, looking back, to have been unusually productive. At such actual or imaginary times, modernity would not be a value in itself, but would designate a set of values that exist independently of their modernity: Renaissance art is not admired because it may have been, at a certain moment, a distinctively "modern" form of art. We do not feel this way about the present, perhaps because such self-assurance can exist only retrospectively. It would be a hopeless task to try to define descriptively the elusive pattern of our own literary modernity; we draw nearer to the problem, however, by asking how modernity can, in itself, become an issue and why this issue seems to be raised with particular urgency with regard to literature or, even more specifically, with regard to theoretical speculations about literature.

That this is indeed the case can be easily verified in Europe as well as in the United States. It is particularly conspicuous, for example, in Germany where, after being banned for political reasons, the term modernity now receives a strong positive value-emphasis and has of late been much in evidence as a battlecry as well as a serious topic of investigation. The same is true in France and in the United States, perhaps most clearly in the renewed interest shown in the transfer of methods derived from the social sciences to literary studies.

Not so long ago, a concern with modernity would in all likelihood have coincided with a commitment to avant-garde movements such as dada, surrealism, or expressionism. The term would have appeared in manifestoes and proclamations, not in learned articles or international colloquia. But this does not mean that we can divide the twentieth century into two parts: a "creative" part that was actually modern, and a "reflective" or "critical" part that feeds on this modernity in the manner of a parasite, with active modernity replaced by theorizing about the modern. Certain forces that could legitimately be called modern and that were at work in lyric poetry, in the novel, and the theater have also now become operative in the field of literary theory and criticism. The gap between the manifestoes and the learned articles has narrowed to the point where some manifestoes are quite learned and some articles—though by no means all—are quite provocative. This development has by itself complicated and changed the texture of our literary modernity a great deal and brought to the fore difficulties inherent in the term itself as soon as it is used historically or reflectively. It is perhaps somewhat disconcerting to learn that our usage of the word goes back to the late fifth century of our era and that there is nothing modern about the concept of modernity. It is even more disturbing to discover the host of complications that beset one as soon as a conceptual definition of the term is attempted, especially with regard to literature. One is soon forced to resort to paradoxical formulations, such as defining the modernity of a literary period as the manner in which it discovers the impossibility of being modern.

It is this complication I would like to explore with the help of some examples that are not necessarily taken from our immediate present. They should illuminate the problematic structure of a concept that, like all concepts that are in essence temporal, acquires a particularly rich complexity when it is made to refer to events that are in essence linguistic. I will be less concerned with a description of our own modernity than with the challenge to the methods or the possibility of literary history that the concept implies.

Among the various antonyms that come to mind as possible opposites for "modernity"—a variety which is itself symptomatic of the complexity of the term—none is more fruitful than "history." "Modern" can be used in opposition to "traditional" or even to "classical." For some French and American contemporaries, "modern" could even mean the opposite of "romantic," a usage that would be harder to conceive for some specialists of German literature. Antimodernists such as Emil Staiger do not hesitate to see the sources of a modernism they deplore in the Frühromantik of Friedrich Schlegel and Novalis, and the lively quarrel now taking place in Germany is still focused on the early nineteenth-century tensions between Weimar and Jena. But each of these antonyms—ancient, traditional, classical, and romantic—would embroil us in qualifications and discriminations that are, in fact, superficial matters of geographical and historical contingency. We will reach further if we try to think through the latent opposition between "modern" and "historical," and this will also bring us closest to the contemporary version of the problem.

The vested interest that academics have in the value of history makes it difficult to put the term seriously into question. Only an exceptionally talented and perhaps eccentric member of the profession could undertake this task with sufficient energy to make it effective, and even then it is likely to be accompanied by the violence that surrounds passion and rebellion. One of the most striking instances of such a rebellion occurred when Nietzsche, then a young philologist who had been treated quite generously by the academic establishment, turned violently against the traditional foundations of his own discipline in a polemical essay entitled "Of the Use and Misuse of History for Life" ("Vom Nutzen und Nachteil der Historie für das Leben"). The text is a good example of the complications that ensue when a genuine impulse toward modernity collides with the demands of a historical consciousness or a culture based on the disciplines of history. It can serve as an introduction to the more delicate problems that arise when modernity is applied more specifically to literature.

It is not at once clear that Nietzsche is concerned with a conflict between modernity and history in his Second *Unzeitgemässe Betrachtung*. That history is being challenged in a fundamental way is obvious from the start, but it is not obvious that this happens in the name of modernity. The term "modern" most frequently appears in the text with negative connotations as descriptive of the way in which Nietzsche considers his contemporaries to be corrupted and enfeebled by an excessive interest in the past. As opposed to the Greeks, Nietzsche's "moderns" escape from the issues of the present, which they are too weak and sterile to confront, into the sheltering inwardness that history can provide, but that bears no relation to actual existence.[1] History and moder-

---

1. Friedrich Nietzsche, "Vom Nutzen und Nachteil der Historie für das Leben," *Unzeitgemässe Betrachtung II* in Karl Schlechta, ed., *Werke I* (Munich, 1954), pp. 232–33, 243.

nity seem to go hand in hand and jointly fall prey to Nietzsche's cultural criticism. Used in this sense, modernity is merely a descriptive term that designates a certain state of mind Nietzsche considers prevalent among the Germans of his time. A much more dynamic concept of modernity, far-reaching enough to serve as a first definition, appears in what is here directly being opposed to history, namely what Nietzsche calls "life."

"Life" is conceived not just in biological but in temporal terms as the ability to *forget* whatever precedes a present situation. Like most opponents of Rousseau in the nineteenth century, Nietzsche's thought follows purely Rousseauistic patterns; the text starts with a contrasting parallel between nature and culture that stems directly from the *Second Discourse on the Origins of Inequality*. The restlessness of human society, in contrast to the placid state of nature of the animal herd, is diagnosed as man's inability to forget the past.

> [Man] wonders about himself, about his inability [to learn] to forget, and about his tendency to remain tied to the past: No matter how far and how swiftly he runs, the chain runs with him . . . Man says "I remember," and envies the animal that forgets at once, and watches each moment die, disappear in night and mist, and disappear forever. Thus the animal lives unhistorically: It hides nothing and coincides at all moments exactly with that which it is; it is bound to be truthful at all times, unable to be anything else.[2]

This ability to forget and to live without historical awareness exists not only on an animal level. Since "life" has an ontological as well as a biological meaning, the condition of animality persists as a constitutive part of man. Not only are there moments when it governs his actions, but these are also the moments when he reestablishes contact with his spontaneity and allows his truly human nature to assert itself.

> We saw that the animal, which is truly unhistorical and lives confined within a horizon almost without extension, exists in a relative state of happiness: We will therefore have to consider the ability to experience life in a nonhistorical way as

2. *Ibid.* p. 211.

the most important and most original of experiences, as the foundation on which right, health, greatness, and anything truly human can be erected.[3]

Moments of genuine humanity thus are moments at which all anteriority vanishes, annihilated by the power of an absolute forgetting. Although such a radical rejection of history may be illusory or unfair to the achievements of the past, it nevertheless remains justified as necessary to the fulfillment of our human destiny and as the condition for action.

> As the man who acts must, according to Goethe, be without a conscience, he must also be without knowledge; he forgets everything in order to be able to *do* something; he is unfair toward what lies behind and knows only one right, the right of what is now coming into being as the result of his own action.[4]

We are touching here upon the radical impulse that stands behind all genuine modernity when it is not merely a descriptive synonym for the contemporaneous or for a passing fashion. Fashion (mode) can sometimes be only what remains of modernity after the impulse has subsided, as soon—and this can be almost at once—as it has changed from being an incandescent point in time into a reproducible cliché, all that remains of an invention that has lost the desire that produced it. Fashion is like the ashes left behind by the uniquely shaped flames of the fire, the trace alone revealing that a fire actually took place. But Nietzsche's ruthless forgetting, the blindness with which he throws himself into an action lightened of all previous experience, captures the authentic spirit of modernity. It is the tone of Rimbaud when he declares that he has no antecedents whatever in the history of France, that all one has to expect from poets is "du nouveau" and that one must be "absolutely modern"; it is the tone of Antonin Artaud when he asserts that "written poetry has value for one single moment and should then be destroyed. Let the dead poets make room for the living . . . the time for masterpieces is

3. *Ibid.* p. 215.
4. *Ibid.* p. 216.

past." [5] Modernity exists in the form of a desire to wipe out whatever came earlier, in the hope of reaching at last a point that could be called a true present, a point of origin that marks a new departure. This combined interplay of deliberate forgetting with an action that is also a new origin reaches the full power of the idea of modernity. Thus defined, modernity and history are diametrically opposed to each other in Nietzsche's text. Nor is there any doubt as to his commitment to modernity, the only way to reach the meta-historical realm in which the rhythm of one's existence coincides with that of the eternal return. Yet the shrill grandiloquence of the tone may make one suspect that the issue is not as simple as it may at first appear.

Of course, within the polemical circumstances in which it was written, the essay has to overstate the case against history and to aim beyond its target in the hope of reaching it. This tactic is less interesting, however, than the question of whether Nietzsche can free his own thought from historical prerogatives, whether his own text can approach the condition of modernity it advocates. From the start, the intoxication with the history-transcending life-process is counterbalanced by a deeply pessimistic wisdom that remains rooted in a sense of historical causality, although it reverses the movement of history from one of development to one of regression. Human "existence," we are told near the beginning of the essay, "is an uninterrupted pastness that lives from its own denial and destruction, from its own contradictions." ("Das Dasein ist nur ein ununterbrochenes Gewesensein, ein Ding, das davon lebt, sich selbst zu verneinen and zu verzehren, sich selbst zu widersprechen.")[6] This description of life as a constant regression has nothing to do with cultural errors, such as the excess of historical disciplines in contemporary education against which the essay polemicizes, but lies much deeper in the nature of things, beyond the reach of culture. It is a temporal experience of human mutability, historical in the deepest sense of the term in that it implies the necessary experience of any present as a *passing* experience that makes the past irrevocable and unforgettable, because it is

5. Antonin Artaud, *Le Théâtre et son double,* vol. IV of *Oeuvres complètes* (Paris, 1956).
6. Nietzsche, *op. cit.* p. 212.

inseparable from any present or future. Keats gained access to the same awareness when, in *The Fall of Hyperion,* he contemplated in the fallen Saturn the past as a foreknowledge of his own mortal future:

> Without stay or prop
> But my own weak mortality, I bore
> The load of this eternal quietude,
> The unchanging gloom . . .

Modernity invests its trust in the power of the present moment as an origin, but discovers that, in severing itself from the past, it has at the same time severed itself from the present. Nietzsche's text leads him irrevocably to this discovery, perhaps most strikingly (because most implicitly) when he comes close to describing his own function as a *critical* historian and discovers that the rejection of the past is not so much an act of forgetting as an act of critical judgment directed against himself.

> [The critical student of the past] must possess the strength, and must at times apply this strength, to the destruction and dissolution of the past in order to be able to live. He achieves this by calling the past into court, putting it under indictment, and finally condemning it; any past, however, deserves to be condemned, for such is the condition of human affairs that they are ruled by violence and weakness. . . . "It takes a great deal of strength to be able to live and forget to what extent life and injustice go together." . . . But this very life that has to forget must also at times be able to stop forgetting; then it will become clear how illegitimate the existence of something, of a privilege, a caste or a dynasty actually is, and how much it deserves to be destroyed. Then the past is judged critically, attacked at its very roots with a sharp knife, and brutally cut down, regardless of established pieties. This is always a dangerous process, dangerous for life itself. Men and eras that serve life in this manner, by judging and destroying the past, are always dangerous and endangered. For we are inevitably the result of earlier generations and thus the result of their mistakes, their passions and aberrations, even of their crimes; it is not possible to loosen oneself entirely from this chain. . . . Afterwards, we try to give ourselves a new past

from which we should have liked to descend instead of the past from which we actually descended. But this is also dangerous, because it is so difficult to trace the limit of one's denial of the past, and because the newly invented nature is likely to be weaker than the previous one. . . .[7]

The parricidal imagery of the passage, the weaker son condemning and killing the stronger father, reaches the inherent paradox of the denial of history implied in modernity.

As soon as modernism becomes conscious of its own strategies—and it cannot fail to do so if it is justified, as in this text, in the name of a concern for the future—it discovers itself to be a generative power that not only engenders history, but is part of a generative scheme that extends far back into the past. The image of the chain, to which Nietzsche instinctively resorts when he speaks of history, reveals this very clearly. Considered as a principle of life, modernity becomes a principle of origination and turns at once into a generative power that is itself historical. It becomes impossible to overcome history in the name of life or to forget the past in the name of modernity, because both are linked by a temporal chain that gives them a common destiny. Nietzsche finds it impossible to escape from history, and he finally has to bring the two incompatibles, history and modernity (now using the term in the full sense of a radical renewal), together in a paradox that cannot be resolved, an aporia that comes very close to describing the predicament of our own present modernity:

> For the impulse that stands behind our history-oriented education—in radical inner contradiction to the spirit of a "new time" or a "modern spirit"—must in turn be understood historically; history itself must resolve the problem of history, historical knowledge must turn its weapon against itself—this threefold "must" is the imperative of the "new times," if they are to achieve something truly new, powerful, life-giving, and original.[8]

Only through history is history conquered; modernity now appears as the horizon of a historical process that has to remain a

7. *Ibid.* p. 230.
8. *Ibid.* p. 261.

gamble. Nietzsche sees no assurance that his own reflective and historical attempt achieves any genuine change; he realizes that his text itself can be nothing but another historical document,[9] and finally he has to delegate the power of renewal and modernity to a mythical entity called "youth" to which he can only recommend the effort of self-knowledge that has brought him to his own abdication.

The bad faith implied in advocating self-knowledge to a younger generation, while demanding from this generation that it act blindly, out of a self-forgetting that one is unwilling or unable to achieve oneself, forms a pattern all too familiar in our own experience to need comment. In this way Nietzsche, at this early point in his career, copes with a paradox that his thought has revealed with impressive clarity: Modernity and history relate to each other in a curiously contradictory way that goes beyond antithesis or opposition. If history is not to become sheer regression or paralysis, it depends on modernity for its duration and renewal; but modernity cannot assert itself without being at once swallowed up and reintegrated into a regressive historical process. Nietzsche offers no real escape out of a predicament in which we readily recognize the mood of our own modernity. Modernity and history seem condemned to being linked together in a self-destroying union that threatens the survival of both.

If we see in this paradoxical condition a diagnosis of our own modernity, then literature has always been essentially modern. Nietzsche was speaking of life and of culture in general, of modernity and history as they appear in all human enterprises in the most general sense possible. The problem becomes more intricate when it is restricted to literature. Here we are dealing with an activity that necessarily contains, within its own specificity, the very contradiction that Nietzsche discovered at the endpoint of his rebellion against a historically minded culture. Regardless of historical or cultural conditions, beyond the reach of educational or moral imperatives, the modernity of literature confronts us at all times with an unsolvable paradox. On the one hand, literature has a constitutive affinity with action, with the unmediated, free

9. *Ibid.* p. 277.

act that knows no past; some of the impatience of Rimbaud or Artaud echoes in all literary texts, no matter how serene and detached they may seem. The historian, in his function as historian, can remain quite remote from the collective acts he records; his language and the events that the language denotes are clearly distinct entities. But the writer's language is to some degree the product of his own action; he is both the historian and the agent of his own language. The ambivalence of writing is such that it can be considered both an act and an interpretative process that follows after an act with which it cannot coincide. As such, it both affirms and denies its own nature or specificity. Unlike the historian, the writer remains so closely involved with action that he can never free himself of the temptation to destroy whatever stands between him and his deed, especially the temporal distance that makes him dependent on an earlier past. The appeal of modernity haunts all literature. It is revealed in numberless images and emblems that appear at all periods—in the obsession with a *tabula rasa*, with new beginnings—that finds recurrent expression in all forms of writing. No true account of literary language can bypass this persistent temptation of literature to fulfill itself in a single moment. The temptation of immediacy is constitutive of a literary consciousness and has to be included in a definition of the specificity of literature.

The manner in which this specificity asserts itself, however, the form of its actual manifestation, is curiously oblique and confusing. Often in the course of literary history writers openly assert their commitment to modernity thus conceived. Yet whenever this happens, a curious logic that seems almost uncontrolled, a necessity inherent in the nature of the problem rather than in the will of the writer, directs their utterance away from their avowed purpose. Assertions of literary modernity often end up by putting the possibility of being modern seriously into question. But precisely because this discovery goes against an original commitment that cannot simply be dismissed as erroneous, it never gets stated outright, but hides instead behind rhetorical devices of language that disguise and distort what the writer is actually saying, perhaps in contrast to what he meant to say. Hence the need for the interpreter of such texts to respond to levels of meaning not immediately obvious. The very presence of such complexities indicates the existence of a special problem: How is it that a specific and important feature of a literary consciousness, its desire for modernity, seems to lead outside literature into something that no longer shares this specificity, thus forcing the writer to undermine his own assertions in order to remain faithful to his vocation?

It is time to clarify what we are trying to convey with some examples taken from texts that openly plead the cause of modernity. Many, but by no means all, of these texts are written by people who stand outside literature from the start, either because they instinctively tend toward the interpretative distance of the historian, or because they incline toward a form of action no longer linked to language. During the quarrel between the Ancients and the Moderns, the debate between a traditional conception of literature and modernity that took place in France near the end of the seventeenth century and that is still considered by some[10] as the starting point of a "modern" sense of history, it is striking that the modern camp not only contained men of slighter literary talent, but that their arguments against classical literature were often simply against literature as such. The nature of the debate forced the participants to make comparative critical evaluations of ancient versus contemporary writing; it obliged them to offer something resembling readings of passages in Homer, Pindar, or Theocritus. Although no one covered himself with critical glory in the performance of this task—mainly because the powerful imperative of decorum (*bienséance*) tends to become a particularly opaque screen that stands between the antique text and the classical reading[11]—the partisans of the Ancients still performed a great deal better than the pro-moderns. If one compares the remarks of a "moderne" such as Charles Perrault on Homer or his application in 1688 of seventeenth-century *bienséance* to Hellenic texts in

10. See, for example, Werner Krauss, "Cartaud de la Villate und die Entstehung des geschichtlichen Weltbildes in der Frühaufklärung," *Studien zur Deutschen und Französischen Aufklärung* (Berlin, 1963), and H. R. Jauss's substantial introduction to his facsimile edition of Charles Perrault, *Parallèle des anciens et des modernes* (Munich, 1964), pp. 12–13.

11. Critical utterances concerning the Homeric question are particularly revealing in this respect, in a partisan of the Moderns like Charles Perrault as well as in a partisan of the Ancients like Boileau.

Parallèle des anciens et des modernes with Boileau's reply in *Réflexions critiques sur quelques passages du rhéteur Longin* of 1694,[12] it then becomes clear that the "anciens" had a notion of decorum that remained in much closer contact with literature, including its constitutive impulse toward literary modernity, than the "modernes." This fact undoubtedly strengthens, in the long run, the cause of the moderns, despite their own critical shortcomings, but the point is precisely that a partisan and deliberately pro-modern stance is much more easily taken by someone devoid of literary sensitivity than by a genuine writer. Literature, which is inconceivable without a passion for modernity, also seems to oppose from the inside a subtle resistance to this passion.

Thus we find in the same period a detached and ironical mind like that of the early Fontenelle openly take the side of the moderns in asserting that "nothing stands so firmly in the way of progress, nothing restricts the mind so effectively as an excessive admiration for the Ancients." [13] Having to demystify the merit of invention and origin on which the superiority of the Ancients is founded—and which, in fact, roots their merit in their genuine modernity—Fontenelle becomes himself entertainingly inventive in his assertion that the prestige of so-called origins is merely an illusion created by the distance separating us from a remote past. At the same time he expresses the mock-anxious fear that our own progressing rationality will prevent us from benefiting, in the eyes of future generations, from the favorable prejudice we were silly enough to bestow on the Greeks and the Romans.

> By virtue of these compensations, we can hope to be excessively admired in future centuries, to make up for the little consideration we are given in our own. Critics will vie to discover in our works hidden beauties that we never thought of putting there; obvious weaknesses, that the author would be the first to acknowledge if they were pointed out to him to-day, will find staunch defenders. God knows with what contempt

12. H. R. Jauss, *op. cit.*, mentions as other convincing instances of critical insight among the defenders of the Ancients La Bruyère's *Discours sur Théophraste* (1699) and Saint-Evremont's *Sur les poèmes des anciens* (1685).
13. Fontenelle, "Digression sur les anciens et les modernes," *Oeuvres*, IV (Paris, 1767), pp. 170–200.

the fashionable writers of these future days—which may well turn out to be Americans—will be treated in comparison with us. The same prejudice that degrades us at one time enhances our value at another; we are first the victims, then the gods of the same error in judgment—an amusing play to observe with detached eyes.

The same playful indifference prompts Fontenelle to add the remark:

> But, in all likelihood, reason will grow more perfect in time and the crude prejudice in favor of the Ancients is bound to vanish. It may well not be with us much longer. We may well be wasting our time admiring the Ancients in vain, without expectations of ever being admired in the same capacity. What a pity! [14]

Fontenelle's historical irony is far from being unliterary, but if taken at face value it stands at the very opposite pole of the impulse toward action without which literature would not be what it is. Nietzsche admired Fontenelle, but it must have been as an Apollinian anti-self, for nothing is more remote from the spirit of modernity than Fontenelle's *perfectibilité,* a kind of statistical, quantitative balance between right and wrong, a process of trial-by-chance that may perhaps lead to certain rules by means of which aberrations could be prevented in the future. In the name of *perfectibilité,* he can reduce critical norms to a set of mechanical rules and assert, with only a trace of irony, that literature progressed faster than science because the imagination obeys a smaller number of easier rules than does reason. He can easily dismiss poetry and the arts as "unimportant," since he pretends to have moved so far away from their concerns. His stance is that of the objective, scientific historian. Even if taken seriously, this stance would engage him in a task of interpretation closer to literature than that of Charles Perrault, for example, who has to resort to the military and imperial achievements of his age to find instances of the superiority of the moderns. That such a type of modernism leads outside literature is clear enough. The topos of the anti-literary, technological man as an incarnation of modernity is re-

14. *Ibid.* pp. 195–96, 199.

current among the *idées reçues* of the nineteenth century and symptomatic of the alacrity with which modernity welcomes the opportunity to abandon literature altogether. The opposite temptation toward a purely detached interpretation, of which we find an ironic version in Fontenelle, also reveals the inherent trend to draw away from the literary. Perrault's committed, as well as Fontenelle's detached, modernism both lead away from literary understanding.

Our examples may have been one-sided, however, since we were dealing with nonliterary figures. More revealing is the case of writers whose proximity to literature is beyond dispute and who find themselves, in true accordance with their literary vocation, defenders of modernity—not just in the choice of their themes and settings, but as representative of a fundamental attitude of mind. The poetry of Baudelaire, as well as his plea for modernity in several critical texts, would be a good case in point.

As seen in the famous essay on Constantin Guys, "Le peintre de la vie moderne," Baudelaire's conception of modernity is very close to that of Nietzsche in his second *Unzeitgemässe Betrachtung*. It stems from an acute sense of the present as a constitutive element of all aesthetic experience:

> The pleasure we derive from the *representation of the present* (la représentation du présent) is not merely due to the beauty it may display, but also to the essential "present-ness" of the present.[15]

The paradox of the problem is potentially contained in the formula "représentation du présent," which combines a repetitive with an instantaneous pattern without apparent awareness of the incompatibility. Yet this latent tension governs the development of the entire essay. Baudelaire remains faithful throughout to the seduction of the present; any temporal awareness is so closely tied for him to the present moment that memory comes to apply more naturally to the present than it does to the past:

> Woe be to him who, in Antiquity, studies anything besides pure art, logic and general method! By plunging into the past

15. Charles Baudelaire, "Le peintre de la vie moderne" in F. F. Gautier, ed., *l'Art romantique, Oeuvres complètes, IV* (Paris, 1923), p. 208. Our italics.

he may well lose the *memory of the present* (la mémoire du présent). He abdicates the values and privileges provided by actual circumstance, for almost all our originality stems from the stamp that time prints on our sensations.[16]

The same temporal ambivalence prompts Baudelaire to couple any evocation of the present with terms such as "représentation," "mémoire," or even "temps," all opening perspectives of distance and difference within the apparent uniqueness of the instant. Yet his modernity too, like Nietzsche's, is a forgetting or a suppression of anteriority. The human figures that epitomize modernity are defined by experiences such as childhood or convalescence, a freshness of perception that results from a slate wiped clear, from the absence of a past that has not yet had time to tarnish the immediacy of perception (although what is thus freshly discovered prefigures the end of this very freshness), of a past that, in the case of convalescence, is so threatening that it has to be forgotten.

All these experiences of immediacy coupled with their implicit negation, strive to combine the openness and freedom of a present severed from all other temporal dimensions, the weight of the past as well as the concern with a future, with a sense of totality and completeness that could not be achieved if a more extended awareness of time were not also involved. Thus we find Constantin Guys, who is made to serve as a kind of emblem for the poetic mind, to be a curious synthesis of a man of action (that is, a man of the moment, severed from past and future) with an observer and recorder of moments that are necessarily combined within a larger totality. Like the photographer or reporter of today, he has to be present at the battles and the murders of the world not to inform, but to freeze what is most transient and ephemeral into a recorded image. Constantin Guys, before being an artist, has to be "homme du monde," driven by curiosity and "always, spiritually, in the state of mind of the convalescent." The description of his technique offers perhaps the best formulation of this ideal combination of the instantaneous with a completed whole, of pure fluid movement with form—a combination that would achieve a reconciliation between the impulse toward modernity and the demand

16. *Ibid.* pp. 224–25. Our italics.

of the work of art to achieve duration. The painting remains stead-ily in motion and exists in the open, improvised manner of a sketch that is like a constant new beginning. The final closing of the form, constantly postponed, occurs so swiftly and suddenly that it hides its dependence on previous moments in its own pre-cipitous instantaneity. The entire process tries to outrun time, to achieve a swiftness that would transcend the latent opposition between action and form.

> In M[onsieur] G[uys]'s manner, two features can be ob-served; in the first place, the contention of a highly suggestive, resurrecting power of memory, a memory that addresses all things with: "Lazarus, arise!"; on the other hand, a fiery, in-toxicating vigor of pencil and brushstroke that almost re-sembles fury. He seems to be in anguish of not going fast enough, of letting the phantom escape before the synthesis has been extracted from it and recorded. . . . M. G. begins by slight pencil-marks that merely designate the place assigned to various objects in space. Then he indicates the main sur-faces. . . . At the last moment, the definitive contour of the objects is sealed with ink. . . . This simple, almost elemen-tary method . . . has the incomparable advantage that, at each point in the process of its elaboration, each drawing seems sufficiently completed; you may call this a sketch, if you like, but it is a perfect sketch.[17]

That Baudelaire has to refer to this synthesis as a "fantôme" is another instance of the rigor that forces him to double any asser-tion by a qualifying use of language that puts it at once into ques-tion. The Constantin Guys of the essay is himself a phantom, bear-ing some resemblance to the actual painter, but differing from him in being the fictional achievement of what existed only poten-tially in the "real" man. Even if we consider the character in the essay to be a mediator used to formulate the prospective vision of Baudelaire's own work, we can still witness in this vision a similar disincarnation and reduction of meaning. At first, in the enumera-tion of the themes that the painter (or writer) will select, we again find the temptation of modernity to move outside art, its nostalgia for the immediacy, the facticity of entities that are in contact with

17. *Ibid.* p. 228.

the present and illustrate the heroic ability to ignore or to forget that this present contains the prospective self-knowledge of its end. The figure chosen can be more or less close to being aware of this: it can be the mere surface, the outer garment of the present, the unwitting defiance of death in the soldier's colorful coat, or it can be the philosophically conscious sense of time of the dandy. In each case, however, the "subject" Baudelaire chose for a theme is preferred because it exists in the facticity, in the modernity, of a present that is ruled by experiences that lie outside language and escape from the successive temporality, the duration involved in writing. Baudelaire states clearly that the attraction of a writer toward his theme—which is also the attraction toward an action, a modernity, and an autonomous *meaning* that would exist outside the realm of language—is primarily an attraction to what is not art. The statement occurs with reference to the most anonymous and shapeless "theme" of all, that of the crowd: "C'est un moi insatiable de non-moi. (It is a self insatiable for non-selfhood). . . .[18] If one remembers that this "moi" designates, in the metaphor of a subject, the specificity of literature, then this specificity is defined by its inability to remain constant to its own specificity.

This, at least, corresponds to the first moment of a certain mode of being, called literature. It soon appears that literature is an entity that exists not as a single moment of self-denial, but as a plurality of moments that can, if one wishes, be represented—but this is a mere representation—as a succession of moments or a duration. In other words, literature can be represented as a movement and is, in essence, the fictional narration of this movement. After the initial moment of flight away from its own specificity, a moment of return follows that leads literature back to what it is —but we must bear in mind that terms such as "after" and "follows" do not designate actual moments in a diachrony, but are used purely as *metaphors* of duration. Baudelaire's text illustrates this return, this *reprise,* with striking clarity. The "moi insatiable de non-moi . . ." has been moving toward a series of "themes" that reveal the impatience with which it tries to move away from its own center. These themes become less and less concrete and

18. *Ibid.* p. 219.

substantial, however, although they are being evoked with increasing realism and mimetic rigor in the description of their surfaces. The more realistic and pictorial they become, the more abstract they are, the slighter the residue of meaning that would exist outside their specificity as mere language and mere *signifiant*. The last theme that Baudelaire evokes, that of the carriages, has nothing whatever to do with the facticity of the carriage—although Baudelaire insists that in the paintings by Constantin Guys "the entire structure of the carriage-body is perfectly orthodox: every part is in its place and nothing needs to be corrected." [19] The substantial, thematic *meaning* of the carriage as such, however, has disappeared:

> Regardless of attitude and position, regardless of the speed at which it is launched, a carriage, like a ship, receives from its motion a mysteriously complex graceful air, very hard to capture in short-hand (très difficile à sténographier). The pleasure that the artist's eye derives from it is drawn, or so it seems, from the sequence of geometrical figures that this already so complicated object engenders successively and swiftly in space.[20]

What is here being stenographed is the movement by which, in apparent and metaphorical succession, literature first moves away from itself and then returns. All that remains of the theme is a mere outline, less than a sketch, a time-arabesque rather than a figure. The carriage has been allegorized into nothingness and exists as the purely temporal vibration of a successive movement that has only linguistic existence—for nothing is more radically metaphorical than the expression "figures géométriques" that Baudelaire is compelled to use to make himself understood. But that he wants to be understood, and not misunderstood in the belief that this geometry would have recourse to anything that is not language, is clear from its implied identification with a mode of writing. The *stenos* in the word stenography, meaning narrow, could be used to designate the confinement of literature within its own boundaries, its dependence on duration and repetition that

19. *Ibid.* p. 259.
20. *Ibid.*

Baudelaire experienced as a curse. But the fact that the word designates a form of writing indicates the compulsion to return to a literary mode of being, as a form of language that knows itself to be mere repetition, mere fiction and allegory, forever unable to participate in the spontaneity of action or modernity.

The movement of this text—that could be shown to parallel the development of Baudelaire's poetry as it moves from the sensory richness of the earlier poems to their gradual allegorization in the prose versions of the *Spleen de Paris*—recurs with various degrees of explicitness in all writers and measures the legitimacy of their claim to be called writers. Modernity turns out to be indeed one of the concepts by means of which the distinctive nature of literature can be revealed in all its intricacy. No wonder it had to become a central issue in critical discussions and a source of torment to writers who have to confront it as a challenge to their vocation. They can neither accept nor reject it with good conscience. When they assert their own modernity, they are bound to discover their dependence on similar assertions made by their literary predecessors; their claim to being a new beginning turns out to be the repetition of a claim that has always already been made. As soon as Baudelaire has to replace the single instant of invention, conceived as an act, by a successive movement that involves at least two distinct moments, he enters into a world that assumes the depths and complications of an articulated time, an interdependence between past and future that prevents any present from ever coming into being.

The more radical the rejection of anything that came before, the greater the dependence on the past. Antonin Artaud can go to the extreme of rejecting all forms of theatrical art prior to his own; in his own work, he can demand the destruction of any form of written text—he nevertheless finally has to ground his own vision in examples such as the Balinese theater, the least modern, the most text-frozen type of theater conceivable. And he has to do so with full knowledge that he thus destroys his own project, with the hatred of the traitor for the camp that he has chosen to join. Quoting the lines in which Artaud attacks the very concept of the theater on which he has waged his entire undertaking ("Rien de plus impie que le système des Balinais . . ."), Jacques Derrida can rightly comment: "[Artaud] was unable to resign himself to a theater based on repetition, unable to renounce a theater that would do away with all forms of repetition." [21] The same fatal interplay governs the writer's attitude toward modernity: he cannot renounce the claim to being modern but also cannot resign himself to his dependence on predecessors—who, for that matter, were caught in the same situation. Never is Baudelaire as close to his predecessor Rousseau as in the extreme modernity of his latest prose poems, and never is Rousseau as tied to his literary ancestors as when he pretends to have nothing more to do with literature.

The distinctive character of literature thus becomes manifest as an inability to escape from a condition that is felt to be unbearable. It seems that there can be no end, no respite in the ceaseless pressure of this contradiction, at least as long as we consider it from the point of view of the writer as subject. The discovery of his inability to be modern leads him back to the fold, within the autonomous domain of literature, but never with genuine appeasement. As soon as he can feel appeased in this situation he ceases to be a writer. His language may be capable of a certain degree of tranquillity; it is, after all, the product of a renunciation that has allowed for the metaphorical thematization of the predicament. But this renunciation does not involve the subject. The continuous appeal of modernity, the desire to break out of literature toward the reality of the moment, prevails and, in its turn, folding back upon itself, engenders the repetition and the continuation of literature. Thus modernity, which is fundamentally a falling away from literature and a rejection of history, also acts as the principle that gives literature duration and historical existence.

The manner in which this inherent conflict determines the structure of literary language cannot be treated within the limits of this essay. We are more concerned, at this point, with the question of whether a history of an entity as self-contradictory as literature is conceivable. In the present state of literary studies this possibility is far from being clearly established. It is generally admitted that a positivistic history of literature, treating it as if it

21. Jacques Derrida, "Le théâtre de la cruauté et la clôture de la représentation," *L'Écriture et la différence* (Édition du Seuil: Paris, 1967), p. 367.

were a collection of empirical data, can only be a history of what literature is not. At best, it would be a preliminary classification opening the way for actual literary study, and at worst, an obstacle in the way of literary understanding. On the other hand, the intrinsic interpretation of literature claims to be anti- or a-historical, but often presupposes a notion of history of which the critic is not himself aware.

In describing literature, from the standpoint of the concept of modernity, as the steady fluctuation of an entity away from and toward its own mode of being, we have constantly stressed that this movement does not take place as an actual sequence in time; to represent it as such is merely a metaphor making a sequence out of what occurs in fact as a synchronic juxtaposition. The sequential, diachronic structure of the process stems from the nature of literary language as an entity, not as an event. Things do not happen as if a literary text (or a literary vocation) moved for a certain period of time away from its center, then turned around, folding back upon itself at one specific moment to travel back to its genuine point of origin. These imaginary motions between fictional points cannot be located, dated, and represented as if they were places in a geography or events in a genetic history. Even in the discursive texts we have used—in Baudelaire, in Nietzsche, or even in Fontenelle—the three moments of flight, return, and the turning point at which flight changes into return or vice-versa, exist simultaneously on levels of meaning that are so intimately intertwined that they cannot be separated. When Baudelaire, for example, speaks of "représentation du présent," of "mémoire du présent," of "synthèse du fantôme," or of "ébauche finie," his language names, at the same time, the flight, the turning point, and the return. Our entire argument lies compressed in such formulations. This would even be more obvious if we had used poetic instead of discursive texts. It follows that it would be a mistake to think of literary history as the diachronic narrative of the fluctuating motion we have tried to describe. Such a narrative can be only metaphorical, and history is not fiction.

With respect to its own specificity (that is, as an existing entity susceptible to historical description), literature exists at the same time in the modes of error and truth; it both betrays and obeys its own mode of being. A positivistic history that sees literature only as what it is not (as an objective fact, an empirical psyche, or a communication that transcends the literary text as text) is, therefore, necessarily inadequate. The same is true of approaches to literature that take for granted the specificity of literature (what the French structuralists, echoing the Russian formalists, call literarity [*littérarité*] of literature). If literature rested at ease within its own self-definition, it could be studied according to methods that are scientific rather than historical. We are obliged to confine ourselves to history when this is no longer the case, when the entity steadily puts its own ontological status into question. The structuralist goal of a science of literary forms assumes this stability and treats literature as if the fluctuating movement of aborted self-definition were not a constitutive part of its language. Structuralist formalism, therefore, systematically bypasses the necessary component of literature for which the term "modernity" is not such a bad name after all, despite its ideological and polemical overtones. It is a very revealing paradox, confirming again that anything touching upon literature becomes at once a Pandora's box, that the critical method which denies literary modernity would appear —and even, in certain respects, would be—the most modern of critical movements.

Could we conceive of a literary history that would not truncate literature by putting us misleadingly *into* or *outside* it, that would be able to maintain the literary aporia throughout, account at the same time for the truth and the falsehood of the knowledge literature conveys about itself, distinguish rigorously between metaphorical and historical language, and account for literary modernity as well as for its historicity? Clearly, such a conception would imply a revision of the notion of history and, beyond that, of the notion of time on which our idea of history is based. It would imply, for instance, abandoning the pre-assumed concept of history as a generative process that we found operative in Nietzsche's text—although this text also began to rebel against it—of history as a temporal hierarchy that resembles a parental structure in which the past is like an ancestor begetting, in a moment of unmediated presence, a future capable of repeating in its turn the same generative process. The relationship between truth and error that prevails in literature cannot be represented genetically, since truth and error exist simultaneously, thus preventing the favoring of the one over the other. The need to revise the foundations of literary history may seem like a desperately vast undertaking; the task appears even more disquieting if we contend that literary history could in fact be paradigmatic for history in general, since man himself, like literature, can be defined as an entity capable of putting his own mode of being into question. The task may well be less sizable, however, than it seems at first. All the directives we have formulated as guidelines for a literary history are more or less taken for granted when we are engaged in the much more humble task of reading and understanding a literary text. To become good literary historians, we must remember that what we usually call literary history has little or nothing to do with literature and that what we call literary interpretation—provided only it is good interpretation—is in fact literary history. If we extend this notion beyond literature, it merely confirms that the bases for historical knowledge are not empirical facts but written texts, even if these texts masquerade in the guise of wars or revolutions.

IX

Lyric and Modernity

My essay title and procedure call for some preliminary clarification before I get involved in the technicalities of detailed exegesis. I am not concerned, in this paper, with a descriptive characterization of contemporary poetry but with the problem of literary modernity in general. The term "modernity" is not used in a simple chronological sense as an approximate synonym for "recent" or "contemporary" with a positive or negative value-emphasis added. It designates more generally the problematical possibility of all literature's existing in the present, of being considered, or read, from a point of view that claims to share with it its own sense of a temporal present. In theory, the question of modernity could therefore be asked of any literature at any time, contemporaneous or not. In practice, however, the question has to be put somewhat more pragmatically from a point of view that postulates a roughly contemporaneous perspective and that favors recent over older literature. This necessity is inherent in the ambivalent status of the term "modernity," which is itself partly pragmatic and descriptive, partly conceptual and normative. In the common usage of the word the pragmatic implications usually overshadow theoretical possibilities that remain unexplored. My emphasis tries to restore this balance to some degree: hence the stress on literary categories and dimensions that exist independently of historical contingencies, the main concession being that the examples are chosen from so-called modern literature and criticism. The conclusions, however, could, with some minor modifications, be transferred to other historical periods and be applicable whenever or wherever literature as such occurs.

What is thus assumed to be possible in time—and it is a mere assumption, since the compromise or theorizing about examples chosen on pragmatic grounds does in fact beg the question and postpones the issue—can much more easily be justified in geographical, spatial terms. My examples are taken primarily from French and German literature. The polemical aspects of the argument are directed against a trend prevalent among a relatively small group of German scholars, a group that is representative but by no means predominant in Continental criticism. But it should not be difficult to find equivalent texts and critical attitudes in English or American literature; the indirect route by way of France and Germany should allow for a clearer view of the local scene, once the necessary transitions have been made. The natural expansion of the essay would lie in this direction.

With modernity thus conceived of as a general and theoretical rather than as a historical theme, it is not a priori certain that it should be treated differently when discussing lyric poetry than it should, for example, when discussing narrative prose or the drama. Can the factual distinction between prose, poetry, and the drama relevantly be extended to modernity, a notion that is not inherently bound to any particular genre? Can we find out something about the nature of modernity by relating it to lyric poetry that we could not find out in dealing with novels or plays? Here again, the point of departure has to be chosen for reasons of expediency rather than for theoretical reasons, in the hope that the expediency may eventually receive theoretical confirmation. It is an established fact that, in contemporary criticism, the question of modernity is asked in a somewhat different manner with regard to lyric poetry than with regard to prose. Genre concepts seem somehow to be sensitive to the idea of modernity, thus suggesting a possible differentiation between them in terms of their temporal structures —since modernity is, in essence, a temporal notion. Yet the link between modernity and the basic genres is far from clear. On the one hand, lyric poetry is often seen not as an evolved but as an early and spontaneous form of language, in open contrast to more self-conscious and reflective forms of literary discourse in prose. In eighteenth-century speculations about the origins of language, the assertion that the archaic language is that of poetry, the contemporary or modern language that of prose is a commonplace. Vico, Rousseau, and Herder, to mention only the most famous names, all assert the priority of poetry over prose, often with a value-emphasis that seems to interpret the loss of spontaneity as a decline—although this particular aspect of eighteenth-century primitivism is in fact a great deal less single-minded and uniform in the authors themselves than in their later interpreters. Be this as it may, it remains that, regardless of value judgments, the definition of poetry as the first language gives it an archaic, ancient quality that is the opposite of modern, whereas the deliberate, cold, and rational character of discursive prose, which can only imitate or represent the original impulse if it does not ignore it altogether, would be the true language of modernity. The same assumption appears during the eighteenth century, with "music" substituting for "poetry" and opposed to language or literature as an equivalent of prose. This becomes, as is well known, a commonplace of post-symbolist aesthetics, still present in writers such as Valéry or Proust, though here perhaps in an ironic context that has not always been recognized as such. Music is seen, as Proust puts it, as a unified, preanalytical "communication of the soul," a "possibility that remained without sequel [because] mankind chose other ways, those of spoken and written language." [1] In this nostalgic primitivism—which Proust is demystifying rather than sharing— the music of poetry and the rationality of prose are opposed as ancient is opposed to modern. Within this perspective, it would be an absurdity to speak of the modernity of lyric poetry, since the lyric is precisely the antithesis of modernity.

1. Marcel Proust, *A la recherche du temps perdu*, Pierre Clarac and André Ferré, eds., Pléiade edition (Paris, 1954), vol. III, "La Prisonnière," p. 258.

Yet, in our own twentieth century, the social projection of modernity known as the avant-garde consisted predominantly of poets rather than of prose writers. The most aggressively modern literary movements of the century, surrealism and expressionism, in no way value prose over poetry, the dramatic or the narrative over the lyric. In the recent past, this trend may have changed. One speaks readily, in contemporary French literature, of a *nouveau roman*, but not of a *nouvelle poésie*. French structuralist "new criticism" is much more concerned with narrative prose than with poetry and sometimes rationalizes this preference into an overtly anti-poetic aesthetics. But this is in part a local phenomenon, a reaction against a traditional bias in French criticism in favor of poetry, perhaps also an innocent rejoicing like that of a child that has been given a new toy. The discovery that there are critical devices suitable for the analysis of prose is by no means such a sensational novelty for English and American critics, in whom these new French studies of narrative modes may awaken a more sedate feeling of *déjà vu*. In Germany, however, among critics that are by no means adverse or ideologically opposed to the contemporary French schools, lyric poetry remains the preferred topic of investigation for a definition of modernity. The editors of a recent symposium on the subject "The Lyric as Paradigm of Modernity" assert as a matter of course that "the lyric was chosen as paradigmatic for the evolution toward modern literature, because the breakdown of literary forms occurred earlier and can be better documented in this genre than in any other." [2] Here then, far from being judged absurd, the question of modernity in the lyric is considered as the best means of access to a discussion of literary modernity in general. In purely historical terms, this position is certainly sensible: it would be impossible to speak relevantly about modern literature without giving a prominent place to lyric poetry; some of the most suggestive theoretical writing on modernity is to be found in essays dealing with poetry. Nevertheless, the tension that develops between poetry and prose when they are considered within the perspective of modernity is far from meaningless; the question is

2. *Immanente Ästhetik, Ästhetische Reflexion: Lyrik als Paradigma der Moderne*, W. Iser, ed., Poetik und Hermeneutik, Arbeitsergebnisse einer Forschungsgruppe, II (Munich, 1966), p. 4.

complex enough to have to be postponed until well beyond the point we can hope to reach in this essay.

When Yeats, in 1936, had to write the introduction to his anthology of modern English poetry, in a text that otherwise shows more traces of fatigue than of inspiration, he largely used the opportunity to set himself apart from Eliot and Pound as more modern than they, using Walter James Turner and Dorothy Wellesley as props to represent a truly modern tendency of which he considered himself to be the main representative. That he also had the courage of his convictions is made clear by the fact that he allotted to himself, in the body of the anthology, twice as much space as to anyone else—with the sole exception of Oliver St. John Gogarty, hardly a dangerous rival. The theoretical justification given for this claim is slight but, in the light of later developments, quite astute. The opposition between "good" and modern poetry —his own—and not so good and not so modern poetry—mainly Eliot's and Pound's—is made in terms of a contrast between poetry of representation and a poetry that would no longer be mimetic. The mimetic poetry has for its emblem the mirror, somewhat incongruously associated with Stendhal, though it is revealing that the reference is to a writer of prose and that the prosaic element in Eliot's precision and in Pound's chaos is under attack. This is a poetry depending on an outside world, regardless of whether this world is seen in neat, objective contours or as shapeless flux. Much less easy to characterize is the other kind of poetry, said to be of the "private soul . . . always behind our knowledge, though always hidden . . . the sole source of pain, stupefaction, evil." [3] Its emblem, as we all know from M. H. Abrams, if not necessarily from Yeats, is the lamp, though here Abrams's stroke of genius in singling out this emblematic pair for the title of his book on romantic literary theory is perhaps slightly misleading, not in terms of the poetics of romanticism but with regard to Yeats's own meaning. In Abrams's book, the lamp becomes the symbol of the constitutive, autonomous self, the creative subjectivity that certainty looms large in romantic theory, as an analogous microcosm of the

3. *Oxford Book of Modern Verse, 1892–1935*, W. B. Yeats, ed. (New York, 1936), Introduction, p. XXXI.

world of nature. The light of that lamp is the self-knowledge of a consciousness, an internalized metaphor of daylight vision; mirror and lamp are both symbols of light, whatever their further differences and oppositions may be. But Yeats's lamp is not that of the self, but of what he calls the "soul," and self and soul, as we know from his poetry, are antithetical. Soul does not, at any rate, belong to the realm of natural or artificial (i.e., represented or imitated) light, but to that of sleep and darkness. It does not dwell in real or copied nature, but rather in the kind of wisdom that lies hidden away in books. To the extent that it is private and inward, the soul resembles the self, and only by ways of the self (and not by ways of nature) can one find access to it. But one has to move through the self and beyond the self; truly modern poetry is a poetry that has become aware of the incessant conflict that opposes a self, still engaged in the daylight world of reality, of representation, and of life, to what Yeats calls the soul. Translated into terms of poetic diction, this implies that modern poetry uses an imagery that is both symbol and allegory, that represents objects in nature but is actually taken from purely literary sources. The tension between these two modes of language also puts in question the autonomy of the self. Modern poetry is described by Yeats as the conscious expression of a conflict within the function of language as representation and within the conception of language as the act of an autonomous self.

Some literary historians, who necessarily approached the problem of modern poetry in a less personal way, have written about modern lyric poetry in strikingly similar terms. Hugo Friedrich, one of the last representatives of an outstanding group of Romanic scholars of German origin that includes Vossler, Curtius, Auerbach, and Leo Spitzer, has exercised a great deal of influence through his short book *The Structure of the Modern Lyric*.[4] Friedrich uses the traditional historical pattern, also present in Marcel Raymond's *From Baudelaire to Surrealism*, making French poetry of the nineteenth century and especially Baudelaire the starting point of a movement that spread to the whole body of Western lyric poetry. His main concern, understandably enough in an

4. Hugo Friedrich, *Die Struktur der Modernen Lyrik*, expanded edition (Hamburg, 1967). By May, 1967, 111,000 copies of this book had been printed.

explicator of texts, is the particular difficulty and obscurity of
modern poetry, an obscurity not unrelated to the light-symbolism
of Yeats's mirror and lamp. The cause of the specifically modern
kind of obscurity—which Friedrich to some extent deplores—resides for him, as for Yeats, in a loss of the representational function of poetry that goes parallel with the loss of a sense of selfhood.
Loss of representational reality (*Entrealisierung*) and loss of self
(*Entpersönlichung*) go hand in hand: "With Baudelaire, the depersonalization of the modern lyric starts, at least in the sense
that the lyrical voice is no longer the expression of a unity between the work and the empirical person, a unity that the ro-
mantics, contrary to several centuries of earlier lyrical poetry, had
tried to achieve." [5] And in Baudelaire "idealization no longer, as
in the older aesthetic, strives toward an embellishment of reality
but strives for loss of reality." Modern poetry—this is said with
reference to Rimbaud—"is no longer concerned with a reader.
It does not want to be understood. It is a hallucinatory storm,
flashes of lightning hoping at most to create the fear before danger
that stems from an attraction toward danger. They are texts without self, without 'I.' For the self that appears from time to time
is the artificial, alien self projected in the *lettre du voyant*." Ultimately, the function of representation is entirely taken over by
sound effects without reference to any meaning whatever.

Friedrich offers no theoretical reasons to explain why the loss of
representation (it would be more accurate to speak of a putting
into question or an ambivalence of representation) and the loss of
self—with the same qualification—are thus linked. He gives instead the crudest extraneous and pseudo-historical explanation of
this tendency as a mere escape from a reality that is said to have
become gradually more unpleasant ever since the middle of the
nineteenth century. Gratuitous fantasies, ". . . the absurd," he
writes, "become aspects of irreality into which Baudelaire and his
followers want to penetrate, *in order to* avoid an increasingly confining reality." Critical overtones of morbidity and decadence are
unmistakable, and the possibility of reading Friedrich's book as an
indictment of modern poetry—a thesis nowhere explicitly stated

5. Quotations in this paragraph and the next are (in order) from *ibid*. pp. 36,
56, 84, 53, and 44. All italics are my own.

by the author—is certainly not entirely foreign to the considerable popular success of the book. Here again, it is preferable for the sake of clarity to put the value judgment temporarily between brackets. Friedrich's historicist background, however crude, and his suggestion that the evolution of modern literature follows a line that is part of a wider historical pattern allow him to give his essay a genetic historical coherence. A continuous genetic chain links the work of Baudelaire to that of his successors Mallarmé, Rimbaud, Valéry, and their counterparts in the other European literatures. The chain extends in both directions, for Friedrich finds antecedents of the modern trend as far back as Rousseau and Diderot, and makes romanticism a link in the same chain. Symbolist and post-symbolist poetry appear therefore as a later, more self-conscious but also more morbid version of certain romantic insights; both form a historical continuum in which distinctions can be made only in terms of degree, not of kind, or in terms of extrinsic considerations, ethical, psychological, sociological, or purely formal. A similar view is represented in this country by M. H. Abrams, for example, in a paper entitled "Coleridge, Baudelaire and Modernist Poetics" published in 1964.

This scheme is so satisfying to our inherent sense of historical order that it has rarely been challenged, even by some who would not in the least agree with its potential ideological implications. We find, for instance, a group of younger German scholars, whose evaluation of modernity would be strongly opposed to what is implied by Friedrich, still adhering to exactly the same historical scheme. Hans Robert Jauss and some of his colleagues have considerably refined the diagnosis of obscurity that Friedrich had made the center of his analysis. Their understanding of medieval and baroque literature—which Friedrich chose to use merely in a contrasting way when writing on the modern lyric—influenced by the kind of fundamental reinterpretations that made it possible for a critic such as Walter Benjamin to speak about sixteenth-century literature and about Baudelaire in closely similar terms, allows them to describe Friedrich's *Entrealisierung* and *Entpersönlichung* with new stylistic rigor. The traditional term of allegory that Benjamin, perhaps more than anyone else in Germany, helped to restore to some of its full implications is frequently used by them to describe a tension within the language that can no longer be modeled on the subject-object relationships derived from experiences of perception, or from theories of the imagination derived from perception. In an earlier essay, Benjamin had suggested that "the intensity of the interrelationship between the perceptual and the intellectual element" [6] be made the main concern of the interpreter of poetry. This indicates that the assumed correspondence between meaning and object is put into question. From this point on, the very presence of any outward object can become superfluous, and, in an important article published in 1960, H. R. Jauss characterizes an allegorical style as "beauté inutile," the absence of any reference to an exterior reality of which it would be the sign. The "disappearance of the object" has become the main theme.[7] This development is seen as a historical process that can be more or less accurately dated: in the field of lyric poetry, Baudelaire is still named as the originator of a modern allegorical style. Friedrich's historical pattern survives, though now based on linguistic and rhetorical rather than on superficially sociological considerations. A student of Jauss, Karlheinz Stierle, tries to document this scheme in a consecutive reading of three poems by Nerval, Mallarmé, and Rimbaud, showing the gradual process of irrealization dialectically at work in these three texts.[8]

Stierle's detailed reading of a late and difficult sonnet by Mallarmé can serve as a model for the discussion of the idées reçues that this group of scholars still shares with Friedrich, all political appearances to the contrary. His interpretation of the Tombeau de Verlaine—chronologically though not stylistically perhaps Mal-

6. ". . . die Intensität der Verbundenheit der anschaulichen und der geistigen Elemente." Walter Benjamin, "Zwei Gedichte von Hölderlin," in Schriften, II (Frankfurt a. M., 1955), p. 377.
7. Hans Robert Jauss, "Zur Frage der Struktureinheit älterer und moderner Lyrik," GRM, XLI (1960), p. 266.
8. Karlheinz Stierle, "Möglichkeiten des dunklen Stils in den Anfängen moderner Lyrik in Frankreich," in Lyrik als Paradigma der Moderne, pp. 157–94. My argument is more polemical in tone than in substance. Some of the doubts expressed about the possibilty of a nonrepresentational poetry are conceded by K. Stierle himself in a later addition to his original paper (ibid. pp. 193–94). The possibility of complete "irrealization" asserted in the analysis of the Mallarmé text is thus put into question. Rather than by the contrast between literature and painting suggested by Stierle, I approach the problem in terms of a contrast between a genetic concept of literary history and modernity.

larmé's last text—following Benjamin's dictum, consciously ana-
lyzes the obscurity of the poem and the resistance of its diction
to a definitive meaning or set of meanings, as the interpenetration
between intellectual and perceptual elements. And Stierle comes
to the conclusion that, at least in certain lines of the poem, the
sensory elements have entirely vanished. At the beginning of the
sonnet, an actual object—a tombstone—is introduced:

> Le noir roc courroucé que la bise le roule

but this actual object, according to Stierle, is "at once transcended
into irreality by a movement that cannot be represented." As for
the second stanza, "it can no longer be referred to an exterior reality." Although Mallarmé's poetry, more than any other (including
Baudelaire's or Nerval's), uses objects rather than subjective feelings or inward emotions, this apparent return to objects (*Vergegen-
ständlichung*), far from augmenting our sense of reality, of language adequately representing the object, is in fact a subtle and
successful strategy to achieve complete irreality. The logic of the
relationships that exist between the various objects in the poem
is no longer based on the logic of nature or of representation, but
on a purely intellectual and allegorical logic decreed and maintained by the poet in total defiance of natural events. "The situation of the poem," writes Stierle, referring to the dramatic action
that takes place between the various "things" that appear in it,

> can no longer be represented in sensory terms. . . . If we
> consider, not the object but that which makes it unreal, then
> this is a poetry of allegorical reification (*Vergegenständ-
> lichung*). One is struck most of all by the nonrepresentability
> of what is assumedly being shown: the stone rolling by its own
> will. . . . In traditonal allegory, the function of the concrete
> image was to make the meaning stand out more vividly. The
> *sensus allegoricus,* as a concrete representation, acquired a
> new clarity. But for Mallarmé the concrete image no longer
> leads to a clearer vision. The unity reached on the level of
> the object can no longer be represented. And it is precisely
> this unreal constellation that is intended as the product of
> the poetic activity.

This particular Mallarméan strategy is seen as a development leading beyond Baudelaire, whose allegory is still centered on a subject and is psychologically motivated. Mallarmé's modernity stems from the impersonality of an allegorical (i.e., nonrepresentational) diction entirely freed from a subject. The historical continuity from Baudelaire to Mallarmé follows a genetic movement of gradual allegorization and depersonalization.

The test of such a theory has to be found in the quality of the exegetic work performed by it proponent. Returning to the text, we can confine ourselves to one or two of the key words that play an important part in Stierle's argument. First of all, the word "roc" in the first line:

Le noir roc courroucé que la bise le roule

The movement of this rock, driven by the cold north wind, is said by Stierle to be "at once" beyond representation. As we know from the actual occasion for which the poem was written and which is alluded to in the title, as well as from the other *Tombeaux* poems of Mallarmé on Poe, Gautier, and Baudelaire, this rock indeed represents the monument of Verlaine's grave around which a group of writers gathered to celebrate the first anniversary of his death. The thought that such a stone could be made to move by the sheer force of the wind, and that it could then be halted (or an attempt be made to halt it) by applying hands to it ("Ne s'arrêtera ni sous de pieuses mains/Tâtant sa ressemblance avec les maux humains"), is indeed absurd from a representational point of view. Equally absurd is the pseudo-representational phrase that combines a literal action ("tâter") with an abstraction ("la ressemblance"), made more unreal yet because the resemblance is in its turn to something general and abstract ("la ressemblance avec les maux humains"). We are supposed to touch not a stone but the resemblance of a stone, wandering about driven by the wind, to a human emotion. Stierle certainly seems to have a point when he characterizes this dramatic "situation" as beyond representation.

But why should the significance of "roc" be restricted to one single meaning? At the furthest remove from the literal reading, we can think of the rock in purely emblematic terms as the stone miraculously removed from the grave of a sacrificial figure and allowing for the metamorphosis of Christ from an earthly into a heavenly body; such a miracle could easily be accomplished by an allegorical, divine wind. There is nothing farfetched in such a reference. The circumstance of the poem is precisely the "empty tomb" (to quote Yeats) that honors the spiritual entity of Verlaine's work and not his bodily remains. Verlaine himself, in *Sagesse,* singled out by Mallarmé as his most important work,[9] constantly sees his own destiny as an *Imitatio Christi* and, at his death, much was made of the redeeming virtue of suffering for the repenting sinner. In Mallarmé's short prose texts on Verlaine, one senses his irritation with a facile Christianization of the poet, left to die in poverty and scorned as the alchoholic tramp that he was during his lifetime, but whose destiny becomes overnight a lesson in Christian redemption. This sentimental rehabilitation of Verlaine as a Christ figure, alluded to in the reference to the miracle of the Ascension, making his death exemplary for the suffering of all mankind, goes directly against Mallarmé's own conception of poetic immortality. The real movement of the work, its future destiny and correct understanding, will not be halted ("ne s'arrêtera pas") by such hypocritical piety. The opposition against a conventional Christian notion of death as redemption, a theme that recurs constantly in all the *Tombeaux* poems with their undeniable Masonic overtones, is introduced from the start by an emblematic reading of "roc" as an allusion to Scripture.[10]

What concerns us must for our argument is that the word "roc" thus can have several meanings and that, within the system of meanings so set up, a different representational logic can be expected to function; within the scriptural context of miraculous events we can no longer expect naturalistic consistency. But between the literal rock of the gravestone and the emblematic rock of Christ's tomb, many intermediary readings are possible. In another prose text of Mallarmé's on Verlaine (that Stierle never mentions) Verlaine, later called tramp (vagabond) in the poem,

9. Mallarmé, *Oeuvres complètes,* Henri Modor and G. Jean-Aubry, eds., Pléiade edition (Paris, 1945), p. 873.
10. The same polemical tone is apparent in a brief prose text written for the same occasion, the first anniversary of Verlaine's death (January 15, 1897) (Pléiade edition, p. 865). The sonnet, which appeared in *La Revue blanche* of January 1, 1897, actually precedes this text.

is seen as a victim of cold, solitude, and poverty.[11] On another level, "roc" can then designate Verlaine himself, whose dark and hulking shape can without too much visual effort be seen as a "noir roc." And the black object driven by a cold wind in the month of January suggests still another meaning: that of a dark cloud. In Mallarmé's poems of this period (one thinks of *Un Coup de Dés*, of "A la nue accablante tu," etc.) the cloud symbolism plays a prominent part and would almost have to enter into the symbolic paraphernalia of any poem—since Mallarmé strives for the inclusion of his entire symbolic apparatus in each text, however brief it may be. The hidden cloud imagery in this sonnet, first perceived by the intuitive but astute Mallarmé reader Thibaudet in a commentary on the poem, which Stierle mentions,[12] reappears in the second stanza and completes the cosmic symbolic system that starts out "here" ("ici," in line 5), on this pastoral earth, and ascends, by way of the cloud, to the highest hierarchy of the star in line 7: ". . . l'astre mûri des lendemains/Dont un scintillement argentera les foules." With a little ingenuity, more meanings still could be added, always bearing in mind the auto-exegetic symbolic vocabulary that Mallarmé has developed by this time: thus the word "roule," written in 1897, suggests a cross-reference to the rolling of the dice in *Un Coup de Dés*, making the "roc" into a symbolical equivalent of the dice. And so on: the more relevant symbolic meanings one can discover, the closer one comes to the spirit of Mallarmé's metaphorical play in his later vocabulary.

"Noir roc" for a cloud may seem visually farfetched and forced, but it is not visually absurd. The process that takes us from the literal rock to Verlaine, to a cloud and the tomb of Christ, in an

11. "La solitude, le froid, l'inélégance et la pénurie d'ordinaire composent le sort qu'encourt l'enfant . . . marchant en l'existence selon sa divinité . . ." (Pléiade edition, p. 511). This text was written at the time of Verlaine's death (January 9, 1896) and predates the sonnet by one year. Gardner Davies (*Les Poèmes commémoratifs de Mallarmé, essai d'exégèse raisonné* [Paris, 1950], p. 191) quotes the passage as a gloss on "maux humains" in line 3 but states, without further evidence, that the tombstone unambiguously represents Verlaine (p. 189).

12. Stierle, p. 174. The reference is to A. Thibaudet, *La Poésie de Stéphane Mallarmé* (Paris, 1926), pp. 307–8. The same passage from Thibaudet is quoted by Emilie Noulet, *Vingt poèmes de Stéphane Mallarmé* (Paris, 1967), p. 259, whose commentary on this poem generally follows Davies.

ascending curve from earth to heaven, has a certain representational, naturalistic consistency. We easily recognize it for the traditional poetic *topos* that it is, a metamorphosis, with exactly the
degree of naturalistic verisimilitude that one would have to expect
in this case. The entire poem is in fact a poem about a metamorphosis, the change brought about by death that transformed the
actual person Verlaine into the intellectual abstraction of his work,
"tel qu'en lui-même enfin l'éternité le change," with emphasis on
the metamorphosis implied in "change." Confining himself to
the single literal meaning of "roc," Stierle can rightly say that no
representational element is at play in the text, but he also has
to lose the main part of the meaning. A considerable extension of
meaning, consistent with the thematic concerns of Mallarmé's
other works of the same period, is brought about by allowing for
the metamorphosis of one object into a number of other symbolic
referents. Regardless of the final importance or value of Mallarmé's
poetry as *statement,* the semantic plurality has to be taken into
account at all stages, even and especially if the ultimate "message"
is held to be a mere play of meanings that cancel each other out.
But this polysemic process can only be perceived by a reader willing to remain with a natural logic of representation—the wind
driving a cloud, Verlaine suffering physically from the cold—for
a longer span of time than is allowed for by Stierle, who wants us
to give up any representational reference from the start, without
trying out some of the possibilities of a representational reading.

In the second stanza of the sonnet, Stierle is certainly right
when he asserts that a *summum* of incomprehensibility is reached
in the lines

> Ici . . .
> Cet immatériel deuil opprime de maints
> Nubiles plis l'astre mûri des lendemains . . .

What on earth (or, for that matter, in heaven) could be these
nubile folds that oppress a star or, if one follows Stierle's tempting,
because syntactically very Mallarméan suggestion that "maints
nubiles plis" by inversion modifies "astre" and not "opprime," what
then is this mourning that oppresses a star made up of many nubile
folds? The word "pli" is one of the key-symbols of Mallarmé's

later vocabulary, too rich to even begin to summarize the series of related meanings it implies. Stierle rightly suggests that one of the meanings refers to the book, the fold being the uncut page that distinguishes the self-reflective volume from the mere information contained in the unfolded, unreflective newspaper. The "nubility" of the book, echoed in the "astre *mûri* des lendemains," helps to identify the star as being the timeless project of the universal Book, the literary paradigm that Mallarmé, half-ironically, half-prophetically, keeps announcing as the *telos* of his and of all literary enterprise. The permanence, the immortality of this Book is the true poetic glory bequeathed to future generations. But "nubile," aside from erotic associations (that can be sacrificed to the economy of our exposition), also suggests the bad etymological but very Mallarméan pun on *nubere* (to marry) and *nubes* (cloud). "Nubiles plis," in a visual synecdoche that is bolder than it is felicitous, underscored by an etymological pun, sees the clouds as folds of vapor about to discharge their rain. The cloud imagery already present in "roc" is thus carried further in the second stanza of the sonnet. This reading, which nowise cancels out the reading of "pli" as book—the syntactical ambivalence of giving "maints nubiles plis" both adjectival and adverbial status is a controlled grammatical device entirely in the spirit of Mallarmé's later style—opens up access to the main theme of the poem: the difference between the false kind of transcendence that bases poetic immortality on the exemplary destiny of the poet considered as a person (in the case of Verlaine, the redeeming sacrifice of the suffering sinner) and authentic poetic immortality that is entirely devoid of any personal circumstances. Mallarmé's prose statements on Verlaine show that this is indeed one of his main concerns with regard to this particular poet, an illustration of his own reflections on the theme of poetic impersonality. The actual person Verlaine, as the first tercet unambiguously states, is now part of the material earth— ". . . il est caché parmi l'herbe, Verlaine"—and far removed from the heavenly constellation of which his work has become a part. The symbol of the false transcendence that tries to rise from the person to the work, from the earthly Verlaine to the poetic text, is the cloud. The misdirected mourning of the contemporaries, the superficial judgments of the journalists, all prevent the true significance of the work from manifesting itself. In the straightforward representational logic of the line, the cloud ("maints nubiles plis") covers up the star ("opprime . . . l'astre") and hides it from sight. In the dramatic action performed by the various symbolic objects, the set of meanings associated with clouds ("roc," "nubiles plis" . . .) denounces the psychological fallacy of confusing the impersonal self of the poetry with the empirical self of the life. Verlaine himself did not share in this mystification, or rather, the correct critical reading of his work shows that his poetry is in fact not a poetry of redemption, sacrifice, or personal transcendence. The *Tombeaux* poems always also contain Mallarmé's own critical interpretation of the other poet's work and he sees Verlaine very much the way Yeats saw William Morris, as a naïvely pagan poet unaware of the tragic, Christian sense of death, a fundamentally happy pastoral poet of earth despite the misery of his existence. In the second part of the sonnet, the imagery shifts from Christian to pagan sources, from the Ascension to the river Styx, with the suggestion that he, Mallarmé, might repeat consciously the experience Verlaine went through in naïve ignorance. Verlaine's death and poetic transfiguration prefigure in a naïve tonality the highly self-conscious repetition of the same experience by Mallarmé himself. Like all true poets, Verlaine is a poet of death, but death for Mallarmé means precisely the discontinuity between the personal self and the voice that speaks in the poetry from the other bank of the river, beyond death.

These brief indications do not begin to do justice to the complexity of this poem or to the depth of the Mallarméan theme linking impersonality with death. They merely confirm that, as one would expect, the sonnet on Verlaine shares the thematic concerns that are present in the poetry and in the prose texts of the same period, including *Un Coup de Dés* with its insistence on the necessary transposition of the sacrificial death from the life into the work. It is important for our argument that these themes can only be reached if one admits the persistent presence, in the poetry, of levels of meaning that remain representational. The natural image of the cloud covering a star is an indispensable element in the development of the dramatic action that takes place in the poem. The image of the poetic work as a star implies that poetic understanding is still, for Mallarmé, analogous to an act of seeing and therefore best represented by a natural metaphor of light, like the lamp in Abrams's title. The poem uses a representational poetics that remains fundamentally mimetic throughout.

It can be argued that this representational moment is not the ultimate horizon of Mallarmé's poetry and that, in certain texts that would probably not include the *Tombeau de Verlaine,* we move beyond any thematic meaning whatsoever.[13] Even in this poem, the "ideas" that allow for direct statement, however subtle and profound, however philosophically valid in their own right they may be, are not the ultimate *raison d'être* of the text, but mere pre-text. To say this, however—and the statement would require many developments and qualifications—is to say something quite different from Stierle's assertion that a language of representation is immediately transcended and replaced by an allegorical, figural language. Only after all possible representational meanings have been exhausted can one begin to ask if and by what these meanings have been replaced, and chances are that this will be nothing as harmless as Stierle's entirely formal notions of allegory. Up to a very advanced point, not reached in this poem and perhaps never reached at all, Mallarmé remains a representational poet as he remains in fact a poet of the self, however impersonal, disincarnated, and ironical this self may become in a figure like the "Maître" of *Un Coup de Dés.* Poetry does not give up its mimetic function and its dependence on the fiction of a self that easily and at such little cost.

The implications of this conclusion for the problem of modernity in the lyric reach further than their apparent scholasticism may at first suggest. For Stierle, following Jauss who himself followed Friedrich, it goes without saying that the crisis of the self and of representation in lyric poetry of the nineteenth and twentieth centuries should be interpreted as a gradual process. Baudelaire continues trends implicitly present in Diderot; Mallarmé (as he himself stated) felt he had to begin where Baudelaire had ended; Rimbaud takes an even further step in opening up the experimentation of the surrealists—in short, the modernity of po-

13. See also footnote 9 in Chapter V.

etry occurs as a continuous historical movement. This reconciliation of modernity with history in a common genetic process is highly satisfying, because it allows one to be both origin and offspring at the same time. The son understands the father and takes his work a step further, becoming in turn the father, the source of future offspring, "l'astre *mûri* des lendemains," as Mallarmé puts it in a properly genetic imagery of ripening. The process by no means has to be as easy and spontaneous at is appears in nature: its closest mythological version, the War of the Titans, is far from idyllic. Yet, as far as the idea of modernity is concerned, it remains an optimistic story. Jupiter and his kin may have their share of guilt and sorrow about the fate of Saturn, but they nevertheless are modern men as well as historical figures, linked to a past that they carry within themselves. Their sorrow is a life-giving form of understanding and it integrates the past as an active presence within the future. The literary historian gets a similar satisfaction from a rigorous historical method that remembers the past while he takes part in the excitement of a youthful new present, in the activism of modernity. Such a reconciliation of memory with action is the dream of all historians. In the field of literary studies, the documented modernism of Hans Robert Jauss and his group, who seem to have no qualms about dating the origins of modernism with historical accuracy, is a good contemporary example of this dream. In their case, it rests on the assumption that the movement of lyric poetry away from representation is a historical process that dates back to Baudelaire as well as being the very movement of modernity. Mallarmé might in all likelihood have agreed with this, since he himself resorts frequently, and especially in his later works, to images of filial descent, images of projected futurity which, although no longer founded on organic continuity, nevertheless remain genetic.

There is one curious and puzzling exception, however. Many critics have pointed out that among the various *Tombeaux* poems paying tribute to his predecessors, the sonnet on Baudelaire is oddly unsatisfying. The subtle critical understanding that allows Mallarmé to state his kinship as well as his differences with other artists such as Poe, Gautier, Verlaine, or even Wagner seems to be lacking in the Baudelaire poem. Contrary to the controlled obscurity of the others, this text may well contain genuine areas of blindness. In fact, Mallarmé's relationship to Baudelaire is so complex that little of real insight has yet been said on the bond that united them. The question is not helped by such lapidary pronouncements as Stierle's assertion that "Mallarmé began as a pupil of Baudelaire with pastiches of the *Fleurs du Mal*. His latest poems show how far he went beyond his starting point." In the early poems, most of all in *Hérodiade*, Mallarmé is in fact systematically opposing a certain conception of Baudelaire as a sensuous and subjective poet—which might well be the limit of his own explicit understanding of Baudelaire at that time—while simultaneously responding, especially in his prose poems, to another, darker aspect of the later Baudelaire. The two strains remain operative till the end, the first developing into the main body of his poetic production, the latter remaining more subterranean but never disappearing altogether. The truly allegorical, later Baudelaire of the *Petits Poèmes en Prose* never stopped haunting Mallarmé, though he may have tried to exorcize his presence. Here was, in fact, the example of a poetry that came close to being no longer representational but that remained for him entirely enigmatic. The darkness of this hidden center obscures later allusions to Baudelaire, including the *Tombeau* poem devoted to the author of the *Fleurs du Mal*. Far from being an older kinsman who sent him on his way, Baudelaire, or, at least, the most significant aspect of Baudelaire, was for him a dark zone into which he could never penetrate. The same is true, in different ways, of the view of Baudelaire held by Rimbaud and the surrealists. The understanding of the nonrepresentational, allegorical element in Baudelaire —and, for that matter, in Baudelaire's predecessors in romanticism —is very recent and owes little to Mallarmé or Rimbaud. In terms of the poetics of representation, the relationship from Baudelaire to so-called modern poetry is by no means genetic. He is not the father of modern poetry but an enigmatic stranger that later poets tried to ignore by taking from him only the superficial themes and devices which they could rather easily "go beyond." In authentic poets such as Mallarmé, this betrayal caused the slightly obsessive bad conscience that shines through in his later allusions to Baudelaire. Such a relationship is not the genetic movement of a historical process but is more like the uneasy and shifting border line that separates poetic truth from poetic falsehood.

It could not have been otherwise, for if one takes the allegorization of poetry seriously and calls it the distinctive characteristic of modernity in the lyric, then all remnants of a genetic historicism have to be abandoned. When one of the most significant of modern lyricists, the German poet Paul Celan, writes a poem about his main predecessor Hölderlin, he does not write a poem about light but about blindness.[14] The blindness here is not caused by an absence of natural light but by the absolute ambivalence of a language. It is a self-willed rather than a natural blindness, not the blindness of the soothsayer but rather that of Oedipus at Colonus, who has learned that it is not in his power to solve the enigma of language. One of the ways in which lyrical poetry encounters this enigma is in the ambivalence of a language that is representational and nonrepresentational at the same time. All representational poetry is always also allegorical, whether it be aware of it or not, and the allegorical power of the language undermines and obscures the specific literal meaning of a representation open to understanding. But all allegorical poetry must contain a representational element that invites and allows for understanding, only to discover that the understanding it reaches is necessarily in error. The Mallarmé-Baudelaire relationship is exemplary for all intrapoetic relationships in that it illustrates the impossibility for a representational and an allegorical poetics to engage in a mutually clarifying dialectic. Both are necessarily closed to each other, blind to each other's wisdom. Always again, the allegorical is made representational, as we saw Jauss and his disciples do when they tried to understand the relationship between mimesis and allegory as

14. Paul Celan, "Tübingen, Jänner," in *Die Niemandsrose* (Frankfurt a. M., 1963), p. 24. The first stanza of the poem goes as follows:

> Zur Blindheit über—
> redete Augen.
> Ihre—"ein
> Rätsel ist Rein-
> entsprungenes"—, ihre
> Erinnerung an
> schwimmende Hölderlintürme, möwen-
> umschwirrt.

a genetic process, forcing into a pattern of continuity that which is, by definition, the negation of all continuity. Or we see ultimate truth being read back into a representation by forcing literal meaning into an allegorical mold, the way Stierle prematurely allegorized a Mallarmé who knew himself to be forever trapped in the deluding appearance of natural images. The question of modernity reveals the paradoxical nature of a structure that makes lyric poetry into an enigma which never stops asking for the unreachable answer to its own riddle. To claim, with Friedrich, that modernity is a form of obscurity is to call the oldest, most ingrained characteristics of poetry modern. To claim that the loss of representation is modern is to make us again aware of an allegorical element in the lyric that had never ceased to be present, but that is itself necessarily dependent on the existence of an earlier allegory and so is the negation of modernity. The worst mystification is to believe that one can move from representation to allegory, or vice versa, as one moves from the old to the new, from father to son, from history to modernity. Allegory can only blindly repeat its earlier model, without final understanding, the way Celan repeats quotations from Hölderlin that assert their own incomprehensibility. The less we understand a poet, the more he is compulsively misinterpreted and oversimplified and made to say the opposite of what he actually said, the better the chances are that he is truly modern; that is, different from what we—mistakenly—think we are ourselves. This would make Baudelaire into a truly modern French poet, Hölderlin into a truly modern German poet and Wordsworth and Yeats into truly modern English poets.

Index